'Our cities are sinking. In the very near future, people will live largely on water. And African cities will be at the heart of this change.'

African Water Cities, 'Lagos Tomorrow' Concept for MoMA 'Uneven Growth' Exhibition, 2014

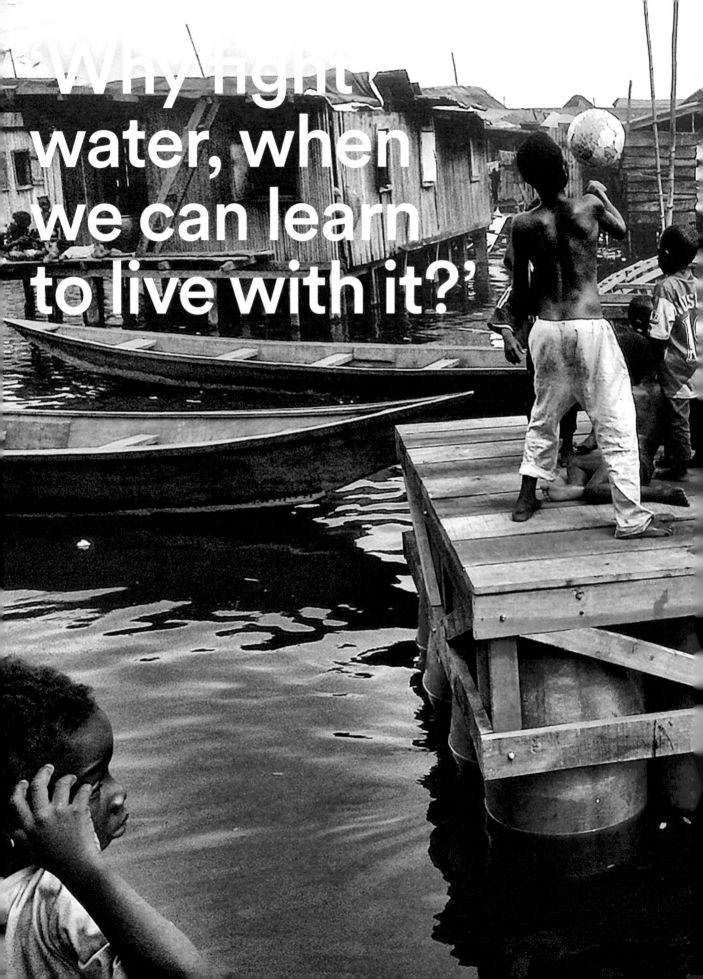

'Why fight water, when we can learn to live with it?'

Platform Prototype for Makoko Floating School, 2012

'Fast growing African Cities face the worst climate risks in the world.'

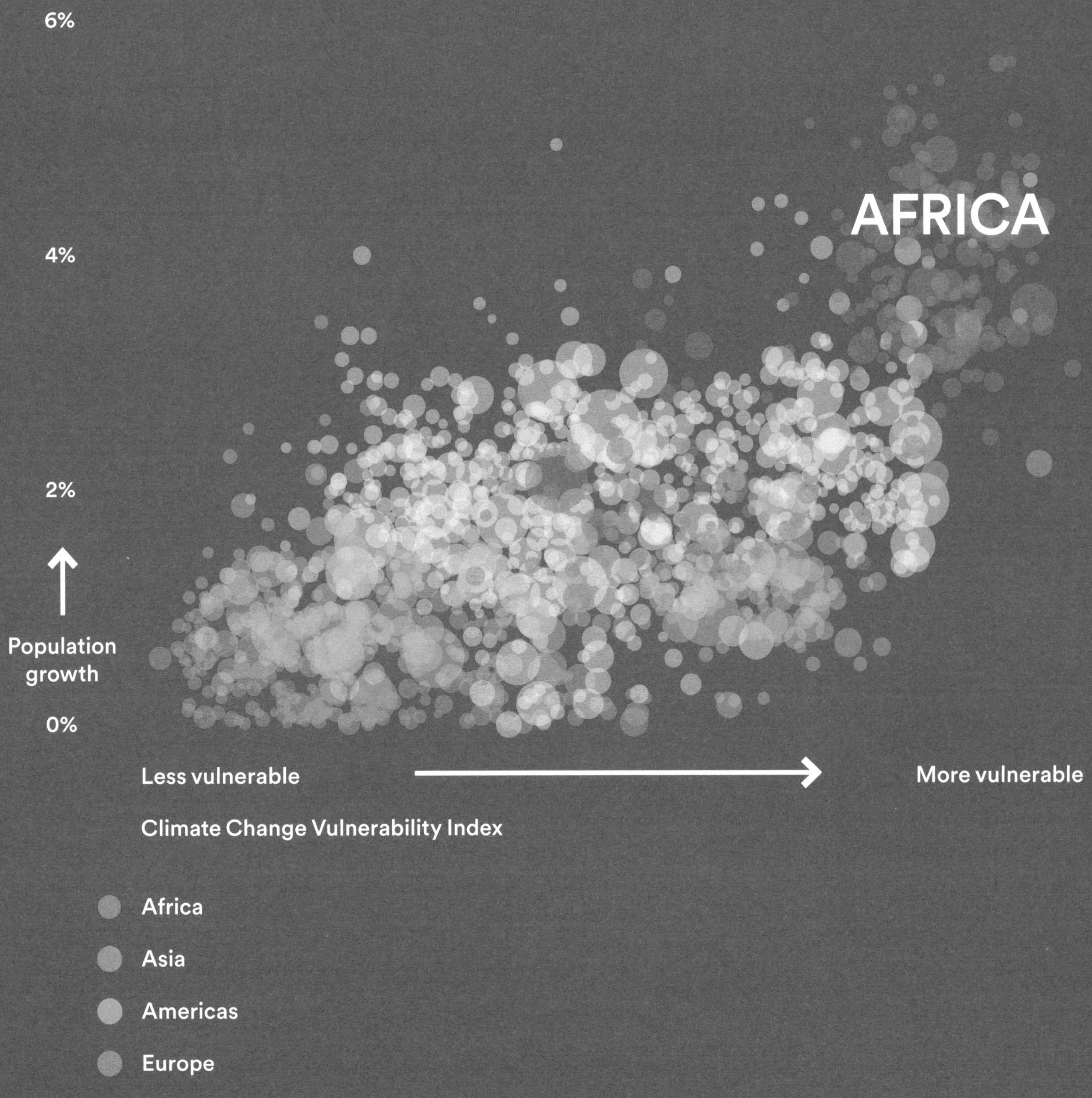

6%

4%

2%

↑
**Population
growth**

0%

Less vulnerable ⟶ More vulnerable

Climate Change Vulnerability Index

AFRICA

- Africa
- Asia
- Americas
- Europe

'Some of the highest projected population growths and climate impacts are on the African continent.'

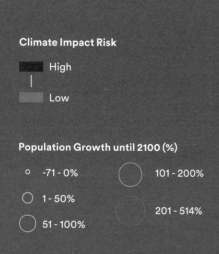

Climate Impact Risk

High

Low

Population Growth until 2100 (%)

○ -71 - 0%

○ 1 - 50%

○ 51 - 100%

○ 101 - 200%

○ 201 - 514%

AFRICAN WATER CITIES

Kunlé Adeyemi

Foreword by Ahunna Eziakonwa
Edited by Suzanne Lettieri & Berend Strijland
nai010 publishers

CONTENTS

Title: Immersion | Medium: Oil on canvas | Size: 30" by 28" | Year: 2016 | Artist: Olumide Oresegun

'Africa is underrated — its true size is nearly a quarter of the earth's land area.'

True Size

Mercator Map Projection

Foreword

Africa's water cities are bastions of action: everything from logistics—connecting traders from the hinterland to markets ashore—to hubs of commerce (in sectors like fisheries, transport and tourism, these cities are magnets) pulling people, especially young ones, looking to turn their dreams into economic reality. Historically, water cities are wealth-creating centres: from Rotterdam to New York, Durban to Dar es Salaam, these cities have been the fulcrum of prosperity—expanding from here to other corners of nations. Often acting as melting pots of culture and entertainment, these cities are also typically the first point of contact with people from outside of the continent seeking to fill their curiosity of what is inside.

The African water cities demonstrate, in strong measure, the paradox of possibility. On the one hand, there is great wealth, as it is here that one observes the vibrance of possibility. On the other hand, Africa's water cities face worse climate risks. And some of the toughest exposure to global shocks, given their integration into global commerce. It is also here that you see the weight of Africa's structural development deficits: as places flocked by Africa's young people, rushing in from the hinterland with valid dreams that often end in disillusion. These very water cities then act as ports of departure, robbing the continent of its strongest asset as young people seek greener pastures far off in Europe, and beyond.

The *African Water Cities* book debates issues: from rising population to rising water, the dynamics affecting life and development in these cities. The collection of essays by expert contributors provides insights into key factors that impact development: demographics, economics, socio-politics, infrastructure, morphology, environment and resources. This is a first of its kind research on such broad multidisciplinary fields synthesized into a vivid publication, presenting in text, maps and images the current state of African cities in the urgent face of rapid urbanization and climate change. The book's deep dive into Africa's top 20 water cities provides unique access to facts and figures from global sources, as well as the realities on ground, offering real experience in adaptation and mitigation and giving us a sense of where we could go. This book is a must-have for city and community leaders, governments, policymakers, planners, designers and scholars as a resource and body of knowledge to understand and develop appropriate responses to the present challenges and future opportunities of African cities by water.

I am proud of the *African Water Cities* vision and would like to commend UNDP's African Influencer for Development, Professor Kunlé Adeyemi, for the fascinating and pivotal work he and his team have been doing for over a decade around the world. I have had the opportunity of seeing firsthand one of the remarkable innovative floating building solutions created by Adeyemi and his team in São Vicente, Cabo Verde. It will take this kind of thought leadership and action to get Africa to rise, not against, but with the tide. And to do so in a sustainable manner that guarantees resilience to shocks while creating prosperity for water cities and communities across the continent.

Ahunna Eziakonwa
UNDP Assistant Administrator and Regional Director for Africa

Makoko Floating School, Makoko, Lagos, 2013

Preface

Growing up in the city of Kaduna in northern Nigeria with my father, Noah Folaranmi Adeyemi, who was an indigenous modernist architect, left an indelible impact on me of a life in nature. Our family lived in an urban home, yet surrounded by a variety of domestic animals and farmland. We had beautiful flower gardens, we grew our own food crops and vegetables, bred livestock we ate and had many pet animals we loved. This may not be surprising, as my grandfather was a farmer. My late father, an architect, was also a farmer. So as the third generation, I feel I'm probably just an architect who thinks like a farmer.

My background shaped my propensity for the natural environment and greatly influenced my work and outlook on life. This may have contributed to my passion for water and the genesis of African Water Cities, manifested through a series of serendipitous events that began in 2011.

While researching solutions for affordable housing for the rapidly growing population of Lagos in Nigeria, I visited the water community of Makoko to see the building and living conditions of what appeared to be a predominantly low-cost vernacular architecture and construction method built on water in the heart of the city. It turned out that the people of Makoko were building some of the cheapest dwellings in the city. They built thousands of lightweight timber houses raised above water on stilts, using low-tech construction methods, with limited resources in an area with almost no land, no conventional roads and no modern infrastructure. During my first visit to Makoko, I was shocked by their poor living conditions and building quality, at the same time deeply inspired by their incredible ingenuity and resourcefulness, to build so much with so little, and their surprisingly happy life. In the same period of July 2011, there was a heavy storm in Lagos that caused many parts of the city (houses, roads and cars) to be completely flooded. I was caught in that flood driving through the city, again shocked by the devastating scale of the deluge, with water covering all that was previously land. In a moment of epiphany, it became clear to me that we were not only dealing with challenges of affordable housing and growth in our cities but also with another significant issue, a force of nature: climate change! And that incidentally, the people of Makoko who live on water were already adapting to this change. If we could learn from them and offer solutions to some of their challenges, we might gain an insight into solutions that address both the issue of affordable housing and that of climate change. The seed for the African Water Cities vision was sown then.

In 2011, my practice NLÉ — still in its infancy — received a kind grant from the Heinrich Böll Stiftung, a green political foundation, to carry out an in-depth study of the Makoko community in view of a concept design we had developed with members of the community for 'Makoko Floating School', our first floating building prototype for climate change adaptation. A building that would live with water and could adapt to its environment. The research enabled us over a period of one year to build relationships and trust with the community. We produced a comprehensive report that formed the foundations of our approach to multidisciplinary research, which ultimately established quite clearly the roots of African Water Cities.

In 2012, NLÉ received the support of the United Nations Development Programme (UNDP) and the Federal Ministry of Environment to build Makoko Floating School as proof of concept under the Africa Adaptation Programme. Its construction was in activism, after parts of the community — declared an illegal settlement and eyesore — were demolished by the Lagos State task force. Our ten-year journey from that point on was filled with challenges, political resistance, criticism, and even threats. At the same time, it has been a rewarding learning experience, resulting from our relentless commitment to innovation, education and action. Makoko Floating School, now Makoko Floating System (MFSTM) has been built in six countries across three continents: Nigeria, Italy, Belgium, China, Cabo Verde and most recently, the Netherlands. It's been tested in different climates, regional policies and water bodies: lagoon, lakes, pond and ocean bay. As is it with innovative processes, we have acquired hands-on experience on how floating systems work and how they can fail. We have learned lessons to make invaluable improvements from a minimum viable product to what is now a standardized prefabricated building system engineered to Eurocodes. The Makoko Floating System is one of many typologies of buildings and infrastructure solutions being developed for the holistic Water Cities ecosystem.

On this journey, I have also had opportunities to pursue this passion for Africa, water and cities through academic research and field studies with bright students at Cornell, Columbia, Harvard and Princeton Universities since 2014. I have shared this growing knowledge as keynote speaker in many prestigious events in over 30 countries. Our work has received numerous awards and recognition, has been in countless publications and featured in many media channels and international exhibitions. Above all, we are most honoured that it has been a catalyst and source of inspiration for the next generation of many young students and practitioners to build upon the vision of sustainable development of African Water Cities.

Kunlé Adeyemi (Prof)
Founding Partner NLÉ / Water Cities

INTRODUCTION

Title: The Space in Which we Travel | Medium: Acrylic on Canvas | Size: 84" x 144" | Year: 2019 | Artist: Calida Rawles

WHY FIGHT WATER?
Kunlé Adeyemi

Port Louis, Mauritius, 2015

Our cities are sinking. In the very near future, people will live largely on water, and African cities will be at the heart of this change. With nearly 70 per cent of major African cities located by waterfronts and more than half of the urban population living in those cities, there is growing evidence that the future of African development is intrinsically tied to its relationship with water, culminating at the intersections of rapid urbanization and climate change. And, invariably, to existential matters of humanity and the environment.

The challenges of water as a resource for consumption in regards to supply and scarcity across the continent is an important and well-covered subject, but the opportunities in water as an abundant environmental resource for urban territory is almost completely uncharted. Particularly with regards to expertise in the sustainable development of cities and communities in the face of water-related climate impact. There is a huge knowledge gap, and the African Water Cities vision triggers the urgency to fill that gap.

'Africa's climate has warmed more than the global average since pre-industrial times. In parallel, the sea level rise along African coastlines is faster than the global mean, contributing to increases in the frequency and severity of coastal flooding and erosion, and salinity in low-lying cities. Temperature increase, heat waves, extensive floods, tropical cyclones, prolonged droughts, and sea level rise resulting in loss of lives, property damage, and population displacement, undermine Africa's ability to achieve its commitments to meet the targets of the United Nations Sustainable Development Goals (SDGs) and the African Union Agenda 2063. By 2030, 108-116 million people in Africa are expected to be exposed to sea level rise risk.'

At the same time, sub-Saharan Africa is projected to account for more than half of the growth of the world's population between 2022 and 2050. With this pressure, governments, communities, developers, and planners are increasingly facing the challenge of expansion of the urban realms, particularly in coastal and waterfront cities. The typical approach to such urban expansion of coastlines and waterfronts is mainly through dredging for land reclamation and construction of major infrastructure to resist water coming into the urban fabric, thereby increasing the land real estate. This approach often has environmental risks and has been reported to adversely impact other unprotected areas and vulnerable communities in neighbouring regions. Furthermore, the approach requires high capital investments for proper execution, which make it only viable for higher income developments. On the other side of the spectrum, there are growing cases of old,

indigenous, and often informal settlements — a rising water population — that are seemingly vulnerable but have surprisingly been adapting to life on water for decades through very simple, natural means. These communities vary in size and population, and can be found in many coastal, riverine, lakefront, floodplains and lagoon areas mostly in South East Asia, and West and Central African regions. African Water Cities unpacks the social, environmental and economic conditions that are enabling these communities and cities to thrive, with the aim of learning from them how to cultivate an alternative, inclusive adaptation and resilient ecosystem and development strategy, specifically for the African context.

Why fight water, when we can learn to live with it?

Land Is Overrated!

The AfDB's 2022 African Economic Outlook report on the needs of African Countries estimates finance needs for loss and damage in the period 2022-2030 at between $289.2 to $440.5 billion. Lagos, Nigeria for example (Africa's most populous city) is one of the fastest sinking cities in the world and it could disappear by 2100… Lagos' low coastline continues to erode, and rising seas caused by global warming put Africa's largest city in danger of flooding.

The challenges present great opportunities to enable people to think differently, to build differently and hopefully to live differently.

The future of African cities in the face of climate change is not all doom and gloom after all. In fact, the African Water Cities' belief is quite the contrary. The challenges present great opportunities to enable people to think differently, to build differently and hopefully to live differently. It is in the DNA of African civilization to adapt to this change. The question of African potential for adaptation and resilience has long been answered, and this book reveals historical and present-day evidence of how people live and adapt in many indigenous settlements in Africa. A question that remains is: what choices will this generation, city visionaries and leaders make to shape the future of a new African civilization? The vision for African Water Cities is one that stands firmly on optimism in the face of realities. One that strongly promotes diversity and coexistence between humanity and the natural environment. It aims to unlock latent potential that stems from our pre-colonial heritage and authentic forms of living in social structures, economic realities, diverse environments and natural resources, in the unique African context. Land is overrated! Water is an asset and a common good. 'If life itself is seen as a future benefit that can be generated from water, then water is, as a result, an asset that provides future life-support services.' We are not alone in this belief, visions such as floating cities, sponge cities and seasteading have become global trends. The UNHabitat says 'floating cities could ease the world's housing crunch' and Forbes described it as 'the next big real estate boom'. Whatever the reality may be, there is clearly a tendency towards developments that embrace water. Perhaps learning from precedents such as Venice, Amsterdam, Chicago and Makoko, where water — an essential ingredient in the recipe of a beautiful city — is an integral element in the urban fabrics of the cities. African Water Cities therefore advocates a holistic approach that embraces solutions that include amphibious, floating, stilt, sponge, and other typologies, into a wider ecosystem of sustainable developments that straddle water to land.

The *African Water Cities* book is a prompt to action. Through years of research, observations, and relentless efforts of innovation we are able to share findings with you by unravelling some of the realities in cities and communities experiencing similar challenges and working towards solutions. African Water Cities research shares extensive knowledge using its custom analysis tool coined 'DESIMER' — an acronym for Demographics, Economics, Socio-politics, Infrastructure, Morphology, Environment and Resources — providing you with a rich collection of photographs, data, facts, figures, artistic impressions and illuminating essays by several thought leaders and practitioners, on the state of the major cities and communities in Africa that are undergoing significant transformations of growth and climate impacts. The *African Water Cities* book offers a window into the ongoing activities, projects and policies at individual, community and governmental levels that will ultimately trigger imaginations, innovations and actions that will shape the not so distant, present, and hopeful vision of Africa rising.

What choices will this generation, city visionaries and leaders make to shape the future of a new African civilization?

Joal Fadiouth, Senegal

WATER LIFE PHOTO ESSAY
Iwan Baan

Makoko, Lagos, Nigeria

Dar-Es-Salaam

Dakar

Abidjan

Zanzibar

Cotonou

Ganvie

Makoko

Ganvie

Ganvie

Makoko, Lagos, Nigeria

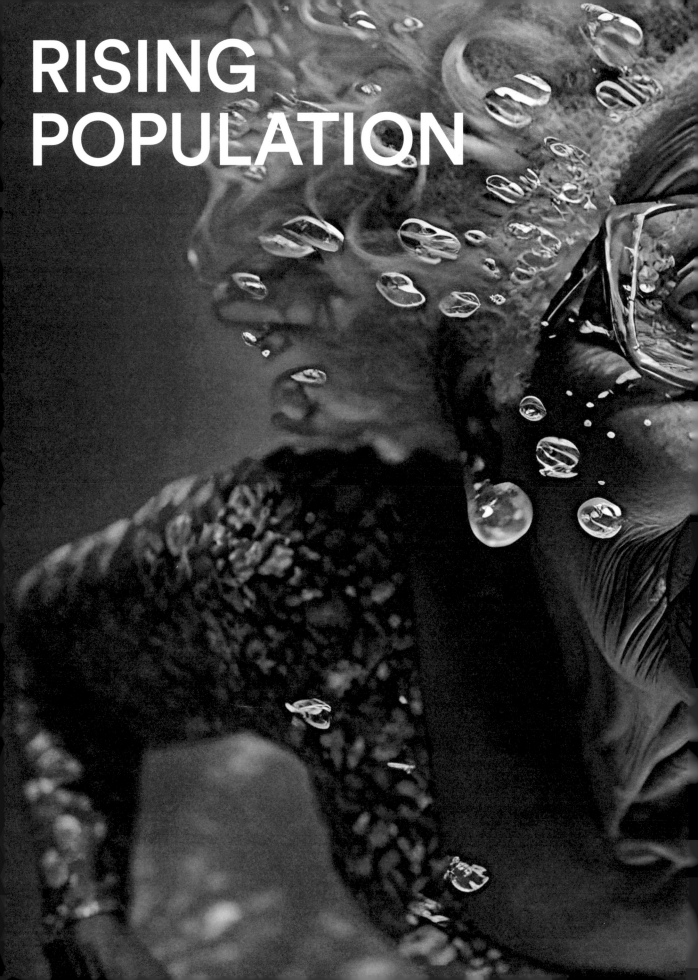

RISING
POPULATION

Title: Nanny Rita Under Water | Medium: AI | Year: 2022 | Artist: Malik Afegbua

'80% of the world's major cities and nearly 50% of the human population are next to water, with most in Asia and Africa.'

+ Capitals
• Major Cities

INTRA-URBAN MIGRATION IN AFRICAN WATERFRONT CITIES
Irit Ittner

Travel by barge on the Congo River

If demographic maps were animated, one would see that people in sub-Saharan Africa moved from rural settlements to urban centres of their countries' hinterlands, as well as to the coasts, where most of the metropolises are situated. Rural-urban migration substantially contributed to the growth of city populations. In addition, urbanites reproduce at high rates. Thus today, urban population growth in Africa is a multi-faceted phenomenon. It is self-reinforcing and depends less on in-migration than before. A rapidly growing number of people in cities require space. Urbanites also move within cities for different reasons, which is called intra-urban migration. The major share of urbanites in Africa are children, youth and young adults.

After national independence, during the 1950s and 1960s larger coastal and riparian cities such as Dakar, Accra, Port Harcourt or Lomé attracted rural migrants due to their economic strengths, the employment and services they offered, and the urban lifestyle. Waterfront cities were often the most important cities, at times even the only large one, in the country. Urban concentration at the coast, at bays, lakes and lagoons, on peninsulas, or at estuaries of large rivers as we find them in many African countries are, of course, not random. Their locations and urban layout carry a heritage from the colonial period, when ports were essential economic and military infrastructure[1].

In post-colonial Africa, waterfronts historically played rather a backyard role for the cities and were underdeveloped. Scholars argue that the historical role of waterfronts as places of violence and oppression made post-colonial city planners and populations generally turn their back to the waterfronts.[2] The picture changed when central land resources within African coastal and riparian cities became in short supply. In addition, the international estate industry turned to Sub-Saharan Africa and also to African waterfronts as one of the last remaining development frontiers. Increasing global competition over investment and attractiveness among metropolises, as well as traveling models of successful world-class waterfront cities also contributed to this trend reversal[3].

Historically, African people, including fisher-folk, dwell *by* the water, not *on* the water. Under special historical circumstances, or under more recent conditions of urban land shortage, communities reclaimed wetlands by different means, or they built villages on stilts in order to make wetland habitable. Most prominent examples in West Africa are Ganvie, a historical stilt village in the Lake Nzulezu Wetlands of Benin; Makoko, a historical fisher-folk village in wetlands of the Lagos Lagoon, Old Fadama situated on the reclaimed wetland of

the Korle Lagoon in Accra, or West Point situated on a peninsula by the Atlantic Ocean in Monrovia. There are countless wetland settlements in those and other African coastal and riparian cities. The coastal metropolis Abidjan, whose southern topography is dominated by the Ebrié Lagoon, wetlands, island, peninsulas and the Atlantic Coast, provides an illustrative example of the specific role of waterfronts in the urbanization process.

Under conditions of housing shortage and high prices, people settle in urban niches and vulnerable locations, such as underused corridors, on the rooftops of regular buildings, at slopes, in swamps and along water bodies.

Wetlands and Unsecured Waterfronts Are Vulnerable Spatial Niches
Water bodies, beaches and banks are defined as public spaces by international maritime law (25 metre zone at inland water bodies, 100 metre zone at the ocean) in order to protect humans from flood hazards, and aquatic ecosystems from negative consequences of habitation. Public authorities are responsible for the prevention of human loss and damage, as well as for the implementation of law.

Under conditions of housing shortage and high prices, people settle in urban niches and vulnerable locations, such as underused corridors, on the rooftops of regular buildings, at slopes, in swamps and along water bodies. Underused public waterfronts constitute a typical spatial niche if water dominates urban topography. After decades of a laisser-faire policy towards the spontaneous urbanization of these marginal, yet central places by the water, West African city authorities rolled out disaster risk reduction campaigns, 'cleaning the city' actions and urban renewal programmes. These policy measures led to the destruction of illegal housing, forceful evictions, and the displacement of poor strata.[4] Displaced people resettled in hazardous locations until they would be evicted from there as well. A cycle began and continued.

In this context, the wetland settlements mentioned above experienced a massive inflow of people over the past decades. Some of them were overgrown by the metropolises[5]. They urbanized while remaining low-elevated, downstream peripheries of their cities, under-served with infrastructure and high vulnerability: pollution, water-logging, high water table, contaminated groundwater (due to leaking septic tanks or the construction on waste fills), water-born and water-vector diseases and floods.[6] Having been established on public land to some extent, and at hazardous locations, poor urban residents in precarious waterfront settlements face the threat of future evictions.

Intra-urban Migration Flows in Abidjan

In Abidjan, repeated evictions and demolitions resulted in flows of intra-urban migrants and a concentration in fewer but much larger spontaneous settlements at waterfronts. Poor urbanites found themselves in densely populated waterfront settlements, where they often lived under even more precarious housing conditions than in their previous homestead.

Triggered by the eviction cycle, the population in Adjahui grew from ca. 3,000 people to more than 60,000 inhabitants (2011-2018). The spontaneous settlement now covers an entire peninsula of the lagoon and hosts a multi-cultural West African population.[7] Ethnographic research showed that three quarters of the 278 interviewed households had been pushed to Adjahui from regular urban quarters and spontaneous settlements from the same or neighbouring municipalities. Thus, they internally migrated within the Southern part of the city. Interview partners mentioned a total of 66 different locations in Abidjan where they had lived before. Some households experienced a series of evictions. Among the eleven most mentioned earlier housing places, ten were waterfront settlements. Four push factors stood out: long travel to the industrial work places in the South of Abidjan (35 responses), high rental cost and lack of housing for newly established households (starters, 58 responses), the demolition of former housing (73 responses) and poverty (95 responses). Demolitions were motivated by evictions from public and hazardous land, as well as for renovation and urban renewal.

The young age of Adjahui's population was striking. Single young men, young couples and families with infants dominated the demography. Usually, a young man wishing to establish his own household moved to Adjahui because he found no housing where he had grown up in Abidjan, let alone affordable housing. Young women followed their partners. Elder people and families with older children had found refuge in Adjahui after demolitions in most cases[8].

> Housing needs to focus on intra-urban migration of low-income earners due to the present and future denunciation of hazardous locations.

Innovations for African Waterfront Cities

In order to respond to deteriorating housing conditions in spontaneous settlements at waterfronts, as well as to increasing risks posed by climate change, planners and architects will need to find solutions to transform the regular city to a more sustainable city that is equally built on social, economic and ecological aspects[9]. The abovementioned push factors to Adjahui hint to some general issues that went wrong in the urban fabric of regular Abidjan. Lessons can be transferred to other African cities with rapid spontaneous urbanization and uncontrolled sprawl into hazardous wetland niches.

In Abidjan, the formal construction sector did not respond to main demographic and economic demands of most urbanites. They are young and living on very low budgets. Demand-driven rental housing for starters and young families therefore needs to use space efficiently. It must be built economically with little resources. The typical city will be much denser. It must offer small secure private spaces, shared space solutions and spacious public places. When families and budgets grow, alternative affordable rental housing in the neighbourhood to upgrade housing status need to be made available. Massive adequate pro-poor rental housing should be integrated everywhere in the regular city, including secure buildings near waterfronts on secure tenure. Housing needs to focus on intra-urban migration of low-income earners due to the present and future denunciation of hazardous locations.

Generally, the urbanization and development of waterfronts in African cities took a different historical pathway compared to cities in the Global North[10]. Challenges and solutions, therefore, need to be contextual. To state it clearly, just another beautiful waterfront promenade and chic waterfront district, as we observe them in Lagos, Luanda and probably also in Abidjan, are not sufficient. We need socially inclusive and ecologically mindful solutions. This requires vision, original new housing concepts, architectural expertise, much effort and finance, as well as courageous city authorities who set up and implement a legally-binding framework where necessary. Their major tasks include preventing the commercial grab of waterfronts and urban waters spaces so they can be designated for public uses[11], such as sustainable transport, education, sports and recreation, climate change adaptation, as well as decent pro-poor housing.

'The world is moving to cities and no part of the planet is urbanizing faster than sub-Saharan Africa.'

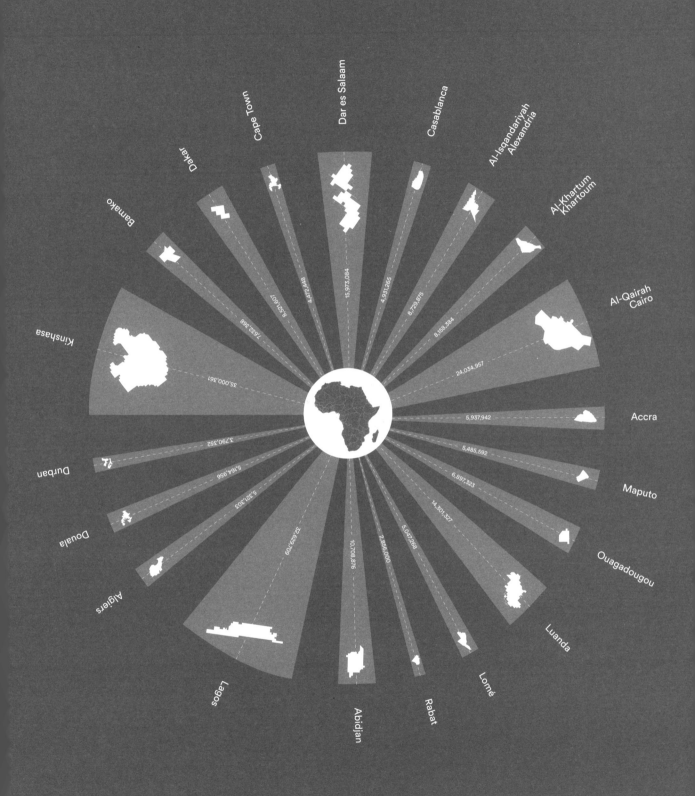

Dar es Salaam 15,973,084

Cape Town 4,472,448

Casablanca 4,931,265

Al-Isqandariyah Alexandria 8,729,875

Al-Khartum Khartoum 8,158,384

Dakar 8,521,607

Bamako 7,635,368

Al-Qairah Cairo 24,034,957

Kinshasa 35,000,361

Accra 5,937,942

Maputo 5,485,592

Durban 3,790,352

Ouagadougou 6,897,323

Douala 5,164,956

Luanda 14,301,327

Algiers 5,121,303

Lomé 5,047,268

Lagos 32,629,709

Rabat 2,856,000

Abidjan 10,708,876

AFRICA'S RISING URBAN AND
WATER POPULATION
John F. May

Fishing boats at West Point, Monrovia, Liberia

The challenges of water as a resource (for consumption) with respect to supply and shortages across sub-Saharan Africa are well known and have been analysed extensively. What is less known, however, is the issue of water as a geographical and environmental resource (for livelihood) in regard to the physical development of cities and communities in Africa. The analysis of the intersections between water and cities is critical for understanding the future of urban development in Africa, particularly as the impact of climate change is now a day-to-day reality on the continent.

This essay will describe the future growth of the population of sub-Saharan Africa and its urbanization trends. Thereafter, the essay will turn to the linkages between the access to water and the socioeconomic developments of urban areas and communities before examining the challenges and opportunities presented not only by urban populations and communities (including water populations) but also by the youthfulness of the sub-Saharan population.

Demographic Background

The Medium variant of the World Population Prospects 2022, the latest population projections issued by the United Nations Population Division in July 2022, assumes a world total fertility rate of about two children per woman at the end of the twenty-first century. According to this scenario, the world population would reach a peak of about 10.4 billion people in the 2080s and would start to decrease thereafter[1]. However, the future demographic trajectory of the world population could well lie between the UN Medium variant and the UN High variant (i.e. half-a-child more than the Medium variant). A similar trajectory already took place in the past decades because of the rapid population growth in sub-Saharan Africa. Should such a higher population growth scenario prevail, the world population would attain its peak at a higher level and reach it later[1].

Sub-Saharan Africa is the only region in the world where the population will continue to increase throughout the twenty-first century. Most sub-Saharan countries, except for those of Southern Africa, are poised to see their population increase by more than 100 per cent during the next 80 years[1]. But the sub-Saharan population is also the youngest in the world. This would change the socioeconomic prospects of the Africa region and its geopolitical weight in the world. Not only would sub-Saharan Africans represent almost 40 per cent of the world population in 2100[1], but sub-Saharan Africa would also become during the twenty-first century the last world reserve of available manpower given the fact that its population would still be much younger than the population of the rest of the world.

Indeed, the demographic youthfulness of sub-Saharan Africa could be its major asset for its future development. Around 70 per cent of sub-Saharan Africans are under the age of 30. What has been called 'youth agency', i.e. a right that allows young people to become the architects of their own future, is characterized by the desire and ability of young people to make decisions and drive change in their own lives, in their communities, as well as in their larger spheres of influence[2].

Sub-Saharan Africa is the only region in the world where the population will continue to increase throughout the twenty-first century.

Urbanization Trends

Sub-Saharan Africa is currently the least urbanized region in the world. In 2022, 42 per cent of its population lived in urban areas (the current proportion for the world is 57 per cent[3]). However, Africa, along with Asia, is urbanizing more rapidly than the other regions of the world. Sub-Saharan Africa is urbanizing very rapidly as well. The urban percentage for Africa is projected to reach 59 per cent by 2050[4].

Currently, sub-Saharan Africa already has many large cities, for instance in Angola, Côte d'Ivoire, Ethiopia, Kenya, Nigeria, Tanzania and South Africa. The number of large African cities with populations between five and ten million is expected to increase, from five in 2018 to thirteen in 2030. In 2018, the region had two megacities with more than ten million inhabitants: Kinshasa and Lagos. Two more megacities are expected to emerge in sub-Saharan Africa by 2030, namely Dar es Salaam and Luanda. Goal 11 of the Sustainable Development Goals (SDG) is addressing this trend and aims to make cities and urban settlements inclusive, safe, resilient, and sustainable.

Africa's Rising Urban and Water Population

The rapid urbanization of sub-Saharan Africa will also increase Africa's water populations. It is estimated that nearly 70 percent of major African cities and capitals are located by waterfronts, namely coasts, rivers, lakes, lagoons, floodplains, and so on. These cities include the following urban areas: Abidjan, Conakry, Cotonou, Dakar, Dar es Salaam, Kinshasa, Lagos, Luanda and Mogadishu (this list includes two megacities and a potential third megacity by 2030). Moreover, several communities and informal settlements in sub-Saharan Africa are all located directly on water expanses. Prime examples are Ganvie (a lake village lying in Lake Nokoué, near Cotonou, Benin), Makoko (an informal settlement in Lagos State, Nigeria), and Nzulezuo (a village located in the Western Region of Ghana).

Challenges

African cities and communities may suffer significant damages from the environmental and climate-related impacts of water, such as rainfalls, floodings, rising water and sea levels, and so on (however, African cities and communities may also experience severe droughts). Because of flooding and rising water levels, these populations may be exposed to epidemics (e.g. cholera) and other water-borne diseases. Floodings may interrupt the supply of electricity, jeopardize public transportation, disrupt access to food, and hamper the schooling of children and the provision of health services. Many inhabitants of communities and informal settlements located on water may suffer from lack of access to clean water and improved sanitation and lack of adequate infrastructure as well as limited access to basic services[5].

Opportunities

Then again, rapid urbanization, including the expansion of water populations, may also offer huge opportunities for sub-Saharan Africa. First, it appears that the population densification in urban areas, including those on waterfronts, is a key driver of economic growth, increasing economies of scale[6]. Second, the massive agglomeration of people is a source of innovation, new ideas, risk taking, and entrepreneurship. The 'nearness', which is also called propinquity, is a positive development factor and historical data demonstrate that better health, urbanization, and income grow together[7]. Third, income growth could be enhanced by the sheer youthfulness of African cities, communities, and informal settlements, as exemplified by the thriving informal sector. Finally, rapid urbanization is also a driving force for countries' efforts to capture a first demographic dividend, which is defined as an economic surplus generated by a change in the age structure along with the implementation of adequate socioeconomic policies[8].

An #endsars End Sars protester wears a mask saying Soro Soke, Yoruba for 'Speak Up!' Port Harcourt, Nigeria 2020

'Waterfronts are often the most valuable real estates, yet the valuation and urban economics of water itself is almost nonexistent.'

Eko Atlantic City land reclamation, Lagos, Nigeria

RISING WATER

Title: Life after MaaSci | Medium: Digital | Year: 2017 | Artist: Jacque Njeri

'Displacement and deaths caused by floods in Africa are widespread.'

**Deaths from Floods
2008-2018 Total**

- ◦ 0 – 163

- ○ 164 – 624

- ○ 625 – 1.859

  ○ 1.860 – 6.433

  ○ 6.434 – 15.003

**Global Internal Displacement caused
by Floods, Storms and Wet Mass Movements
2008-2018 Total**

- • 0 – 363.241
- ● 363.242 – 1.725.650
- ● 1.725.651 – 3.439.643

- ● 3.439.644 – 14.618.193
- ● 14.618.194 – 58.217.125

AFRICAN WATER CITIES

WATER, THE CRADLE AND COFFIN OF CIVILIZATION

Steven Mithen

The domestication of plants and animals is traditionally believed to be the key event in the past of humankind that led to the emergence of urbanism and what we term 'civilization'. This occurred independently in several regions of the world during the early and mid-Holocene: initially in SW Asia between 12 and 10,000 years ago. Then, around 7,000 years ago, squash maize and beans were domesticated in Mesoamerica. When water security failed, civilizations collapsed. Such was the value of water that it became a source of power: controlling the water supply was as important as its management in the ongoing development of state societies and empires.

This is evident in the huge investments in aqueducts, cisterns, and irrigation systems found in all ancient civilizations, those from Ancient China, through Ancient Greece and the Roman Empire, to Central and South America. It remains a concern today, with many of the world's urban populations facing water scarcity, with impacts on health and the food supply. Ongoing urbanization and climate change continue to exacerbate the challenge, threatening future urban livelihoods throughout the world

The most explicit relationship between water, power and civilization within the Wadi Araba comes from the Nabataean culture that flourished in southern Jordan between the late fourth and first centuries BC. The Nabateans were the go-betweens of old-world trade networks, located at the centre of trade routes that connected southern Arabia to the northern Levant and Europe. They built their capital at Petra, located in a basin at the confluence of five wadis, carving monumental architecture from the dramatic sandstone cliffs. The Nabataean centres display burgeoning urban populations, estimated to have reached 30,000 at Petra, with all the trappings of civilization.

This was achieved in one of the driest regions of the world, rarely receiving more than 75 millimetres of rain per year. To do so, the Nabateans developed and deployed hydraulic engineering at a scale never seen before in the ancient world. They constructed terrace walls to capture and channel rain water; barrages to slow water flow along wadis to enhance infiltration; containment dams to collect vast pools of water. Lengthy aqueducts, some covering more than 20 kilometres, were constructed to bring water from distant springs. These fed complexes of cisterns that were carved from the bedrock. Reservoirs were constructed.

By managing the sparse rainfall and deep aquifers in this manner, there was sufficient water to meet the drinking needs of people and animals, the irrigation of crops and the water requirements of craft production, in an extremely arid landscape.

Water was used for other purposes as well. The centre of Petra was turned green by an ostentatious use of water to create a pool of clear water with a central pavilion, filled by an artificial waterfall and surrounded by gardens with olives, figs, grapes, walnut and flowering plants, and a waterfall. This was a display of wealth by the Nabatean kings to impress visitors to the city. It was a demonstration of their power over the most precious commodity within the region: water.

Such was the value of water that it became a source of power: controlling the water supply was as important as its management in the ongoing development of state societies and empires.

INDIGENOUS WATER COMMUNITIES

Historically, people have built and lived on water all over the world, in all cultures, classes, economic conditions, in different materiality, and in different climates and water bodies. The reasons for people to build on water are diverse, and can be economic, socio-political or environmental ones, among others.

Some communities on water are there because of a typical resource that is well accessible by water: for instance, shipping, timber, and fishing industries. As water represents the cheapest form of energy when it comes to transportation, it is no surprise that trading communities have formed on or close to water for the efficient movement of goods.

Socio-political reasons have also been a major driver for people to move to water. Although Venice in Italy and Ganvie in Ghana are very different in size, economy and culture, they have been built for some of the same reasons: avoiding slavery or capture by enemies.

Water-based settlements also exist in places where land is unaffordable for migrants and thus people move to live on water to meet the pace of demographic development. As the economic value of water bodies is not always clear, their occupation has historically not been contested as much as land and was available for development. In modern times, water-based and water-adjacent developments are the foundation of much of recreational developments and tourism, one of the fastest growing industries of our time.

Stilt housing — a universal building typology on water — and communities are built primarily to protect against floods and changing water environments. Alternatively, making use of differences in terrain has led some communities to develop their flood-prone settlements by building on mounds.

In the African context, we look at indigenous water-based communities through different types of water bodies: coast, river, lake, lagoon, floodplain. Each brings unique models for development on and around water.

Ancient African civilisations developed around water bodies.
Pyramids during the flood season of the Nile, Egypt, ca. 1890

Coastal cities and communities — where land meets sea — are at the forefront of natural events such as storms and landslides, as well as longer term coastal erosion and rising sea levels.

Guet N'dar is a neighbourhood in the city of Saint-Louis, in the northwest of Senegal. Saint-Louis is close to the Senegal River's mouth. With an estimated official population of 258,000 it served as the capital of the French colony of Senegal from 1673 to 1902, and of French West Africa from 1895 to 1902 before the capital was transferred to Dakar. Moreover, from 1920 to 1957, it functioned as the capital of the neighbouring colony of Mauritania.

Rising sea levels, as well as water levels flowing out of the Senegal River now threaten the low-lying islands which make up the city. Since 2008, the coast of the community has eroded by 1–2 meters a year and is under severe threat of further erosion.

RISING WATER

River communities experience 'fluvial' flooding due to rapid increase of water runoff or limited discharge, which typically happens in the rainy season.

Monrovia, the capital city of Liberia, is home to a growing population of 1.3 million people. Located between the Atlantic Ocean and the Mesurado and Saint Paul rivers, the city has limited options for expansion. As a result, two-thirds of Monrovians live in informal settlements in low-lying areas along the banks of the Stockton Creek and Du River, including Slipway, Doe Community, Saye Town, Logan Town, Clara and Via Towns, and the famous West Point.

The rapid growth of Monrovia's population, along with the influx of people from other parts of the country who were displaced by the 14-year civil war, has led to the rapid expansion of informal settlements in high-risk areas of the city. These settlements are often located in low-lying coastal areas and swampy, flood-prone land, which poses a danger to the health and employment of their residents. In some cases, heavy rainfall and low elevations result in year-round flooding in these slum communities.

Makoko is a unique inner-city community in Nigeria, with a third of the community built on stilts in a lagoon off the Lagos mainland. The famous Nigerian megacity has a population of around 21 million, and transport in Makoko is mainly by canoe. The rest of the settlement is located on swampy land with poor sanitation and limited access to public services.

Makoko originated as a fishing settlement, with families migrating there from the Benin Republic in the nineteenth century.

Today, Makoko houses over 80,000 inhabitants, and has no roads and no modern infrastructure. The pressures of urbanization have made building on water a viable alternative for cheap living. Fish and timber industries dominate its economic activity.

AFRICAN WATER CITIES

Lakes throughout the continent are experiencing different impacts of a changing climate. Some are drying out, some are rising.

Ganvie is a settlement of about 30,000 people that stands on stilts in the middle of Lake Nokoué. The town, one of the largest lake villages in Benin, originated in the sixteenth century and serves as a home for the Tofinu people.

Known as the 'Venice of Africa', Ganvie today has an economy based on fishing, aquaculture and tourism. Life in Ganvie has adjusted entirely to being on water, with stilt housing, amenities and floating markets.

RISING WATER

Floodplains experience 'pluvial' flooding, occasionally turning a desert into flooded grasslands in the rain season. The increasing water volumes decrease land available for urban development.

Oshakati is an urban settlement within the drainage system of the Cuvelai Basin. The basin undergoes an annual phenomenon, whereby rains and flash floods turn the desert into hundreds of channels that interconnect and diverge thousands of times. For the greater part of the year, the majority of channels remain dry, and any water flow that occurs is characterized by a fluctuation between slow trickles and enormous floods that gradually make their way downstream.

Shallow wells in the region have a consistent supply of fresh water, replenished by rainfall and flows of fresh water down the Central Drainage. Almost all elevated land above the drainage channels and pans in these central zones of Namibia is inhabited as it is the least prone to seasonal flooding.

RISING WATER

NAVIGATING THE IMPACT
OF CLIMATE CHANGE
Hellen Njoki Wanjohi-Opil

Damaged houses and roads after Hurricane Kenneth, Pemba, Mozambique

Water has always been intricately linked with the development of cities in Africa. Historically, many communities were naturally drawn to the most fertile areas, which were those near predominantly inland sources of water[1], such as rivers and lakes, that could support agriculture[2]. Consequently, most of the early areas of population conglomerations in Africa were 'agro-towns'[3]. With the onset of colonization, the African coast experienced the emergence of large coastal cities[4], as they were ideal ports of trade with other continents. It is no wonder that today, across Africa, more than half of the continent's largest cities are 'water cities', situated by water. The most populous cities in West Africa such as Lagos, Abidjan, and Dakar, all lie along the Atlantic Coast. In North Africa, Africa's second-largest city, Cairo, is traversed by the majestic Nile River, while Southern Africa hosts major cities such as Luanda and Cape Town along the coasts of both the Atlantic and Indian Oceans. The case is the same in East & Central Africa, home to both coastal cities, but also more significantly, the largest portion of the Great Lakes Region that has multiple inland water cities such as Kinshasa and Jinja that lie on banks of the big rivers.

Across Africa, cities are grappling with the impact of climate change and the continent's water cities have been epicentres of urban climate losses, and this is projected to worsen. The International Panel on Climate Change identifies urban coastlines as one of the most at-risk areas to climate change impact, also warning that 'climate change risks to cities, settlements and key infrastructure will rise rapidly in the medium and long term with further global warming'.[5]

Today, cities along the African coast are facing similar crises and tragedies brought on by climate change. The city of Lagos in Nigeria, which lies less than two metres above sea level, is threatened by sea level rise, compounded by heavy flooding caused by recurrent extreme rainfall[6]. Successive cyclones have devastated the coastal city of Beira in Mozambique, in addition to saltwater intrusion of the delta from which it draws its fresh water supplies[7]. Climate change has not spared inland water cities either. The city of Khartoum for instance, located at the confluence of the White and Blue Nile Rivers, has perennially been afflicted by river flooding, causing deaths and destroying urban infrastructure[8].

In addition to the losses to human life, infrastructure and ecosystems, climate risks to Africa's water cities pose a devastating risk to local livelihoods and culture. Disappearing archaeological heritage sites and aesthetic beaches in the historical city of Alexandria, caused by the rising levels of the Mediterranean Sea, will negatively impact the city's tourism sector[9]. The town of Saint-Louis in Senegal that is a UNESCO World Heritage site is also losing historical homes and social infrastructure to inundation and coastal erosion, which has also displaced local communities[10]. The bleaching of previously multi-coloured corals off Kenyan coastal cities such as Mombasa, is affecting local communities who make their living from offering boat rides to snorkelling sites to tourists. With fishing being a vital source of income for many water cities, warming seas for instance, are transforming fish ecosystems, and endangering fishermen's boats and homes through resultant storms.

> Today, in most African cities, informal settlements are found along precarious urban riverbanks, which are highly vulnerable to climate-induced flooding and landslides.

While water cities are themselves at risk from climate change, water has also served as a source of differentiated urban climate risk. While there has been an attraction of African cities to water, the informal part of these cities has often been driven towards water by poverty. Today, in most African cities, informal settlements are found along precarious urban riverbanks, which are highly vulnerable to climate-induced flooding and landslides. Cyclical losses to these already poor communities risks trapping them in a cycle of poverty that they are often unable to break[11].

As a result, water cities have remained locations of some of the most innovative climate adaptation solutions, as adaptation to water in Africa is not a modern phenomenon. For over four centuries, the historical lake villages of Ganvie in the city of Cotonou in Benin[12], and Nzulezu in Ghana have existed on water, with structures built on stilts. Today, harnessing the power of nature, the city of Beira in Mozambique has created a natural urban watershed made up of restored mangroves and green urban parks to climate proof the city. Other cities such as Alexandria, Saint-Louis and Mombasa have adopted more 'hard engineering' solutions such as building sea walls in places to protect vulnerable heritage sites. At neighbourhood level, informal settlement communities in Kenya use sand-filled sacks at their doorsteps to keep flood waters out of their homes.

Interestingly, climate change has not triggered a morphological retreat of African cities away from water. As the continent continues to urbanize at the fastest rate in the world, population growth in low elevation coastal areas and along inland water bodies is surging. It is estimated that the continent's coastal cities will grow at more than one and a half times the rate of Africa's total population growth in the next decade alone[13]. As Africa's water cities race to build their resilience to climate change, they must however be careful not to maladapt. Sea walls built without proper analysis of future climate impact, for instance, may increase population and asset densities along water bodies by creating a false sense of safety[14]. On the other hand, nature-based solutions on their own are not able to fully engineer climate resilient African cities of the future, and thus additional risk-reducing infrastructure must be prioritized. Critically, cities must also prioritize building the resilience of the most vulnerable within the cities themselves, often those directly interfacing with water. Finally, robust city resilience plans anchored on strong climate data coupled with expanded access to climate finance will keep Africa's water cities afloat.

As a result, water cities have remained locations of some of the most innovative climate adaptation solutions, as adaptation to water in Africa is not a modern phenomenon.

AFRICAN WATER CITIES

The Blue Nile flooded and burst its banks sweeping away many homes in Khartoum, 1988

URBAN WATER SUPPLY
AND SANITATION
Winnie V. Mitullah

Sachet water delivery in Nima, Accra

Demographic shifts are directly related to environmental resources such as water, which remains scarce in all regions. Scarcity is attributed to population growth, income levels, rising living standards, modification of landscape and land use, contamination of water supplies, and inefficiency in water use. Investment in water has a catalytic effect on areas such as health, education, agriculture, and job creation (UN-Water, 2021)[1] through industry. Consequently, a comprehensive examination of water and sanitation (WATSAN) has to cover the entire water cycle and all its linkages, including the ecosystem from which water is drawn. Cities are at the centre of this equation due to their rapid population growth, prevailing inequalities in service delivery across income groups and settlements, and connection to the surrounding basins from which they draw their water.

Prominence of WATSAN has been shown in global commitments, including the Millennium Development Goals and Sustainable Development Goals. These commitments target reducing the number of people without sustainable access to safe drinking water and sanitation, and ensuring availability and sustainable management of WATSAN for all. Monitoring of SDGs after five years show minimal progress being made on drinking water coverage in Africa, with a significant percentage still relying on unimproved and surface water. This is contrary to global figures which show that 3 out of 4 people used safely managed water in 2020. Almost half of African countries lacked data, and for those that have data, the proportion of people using safely managed drinking water services in 2020 was below 25 per cent, with a few others falling between 25 – 50 per cent (UN-Water, 2021)[2].

> Monitoring of SDGs after five years show minimal progress being made on drinking water coverage in Africa, with a significant percentage still relying on unimproved and surface water.

Water in Cities

Urban WATSAN is a major challenge in African cities, and continues to undermine sustainable development. Water bowsers, hand cart pushers and long queues for water, in particular in low-income popular urban settlements are a common sight. The water stress is intensified by climate change in precipitation and temperature patterns affecting availability of water as manifested in water shortages, droughts and floods. The latter changes the geomorphology of cities, their heights above sea level as well as the price and affordability of clean, bottled water. Shortages affect all city dwellers, but the problem is more intense among the poor who rely on communal taps or water vendors. The quality of water supplied by vendors is never assured and it is often more expensive than water supplied by local city authorities (Gulyani et al., 2005)[3]. Also, the supply by the city authorities is often intermittent, with several instances of dry taps due to shortage, rationing, and technical supply challenges.

The demographic challenge of satisfying the water needs of urban residents is occurring in the midst of many related supply inefficiencies, including high distributional losses, low billing, collection of revenue, over staffing and under recovery of costs (WHO/UNICEF, 2011[4]. Infrastructure for supply of water and treatment of sewage and wastewater remains inadequate, which contributes to the bulk of the 842,000 water quality-related deaths each year. In most cities informal settlements are not adequately covered by water infrastructure. This was intensified during Covid-19 when many lacked basic hand washing facilities and relied on shared toilets (OECD, 2021)[5]. In some of these settlements communal standpipes exist, with services provided through a hybrid system by different service providers. Services are never adequate, and many citizens use contaminated or unsafe drinking water, poor sanitation and inadequate hygiene (Manna, 2019)[6].

Solving WATSAN challenges in Africa remains a priority (Hajjar, 2020)[7] in cities. Privatization and corporatization have been used to address the problem, but this has not resulted in availability and affordability (Beard and Mitlin, 2021)[8] of WATSAN. The challenge is more intense among the poor, while the better-off have alternatives in private services through tracked delivery of water, private boreholes and in-home treatment systems. The poor cannot afford such services and have rely on local authority communal standpipe supply, water vendors and other sources, which are often unsafe. However, the effects of climate change are affecting water sources and exposing the entire population of cities to water scarcity irrespective of a household's economic status. For example, in South Africa rationing affected all households in cities such as Cape Town during the 2019 drought.

Most cities are prone to WATSAN challenges related to climate change, ranging from floods to dry rivers, dams and taps. These events cause WATSAN insecurity with drastic effects on the health of urban dwellers. Apart from climate change knowledge, these challenges require resources for replacing, expanding and maintaining water infrastructure in cities. Most cities have old infrastructure prone to destruction during floods, due to low carrying capacity and inability to cope with stress. Africa has to deal with issues of equitable supply and governance of safe water, and climate change. This needs a holistic approach to WATSAN management, including climate-resilient sensitive planning and management of water resources and services.

Conclusion
The challenge of water and sanitation delivery in urban Africa is intertwined with demographics and climate change, manifested in floods and water scarcity. Cities are rapidly growing with large informal settlements built on areas at risk. Addressing these challenges requires leveraging of resources, including climate change mitigation and adaptation knowledge from stakeholders.

However, the effects of climate change are affecting water sources and exposing the entire population of cities to water scarcity irrespective of a household's economic status.

A young pure water seller

'Northern and southern Africa experience high rates of water depletion.'

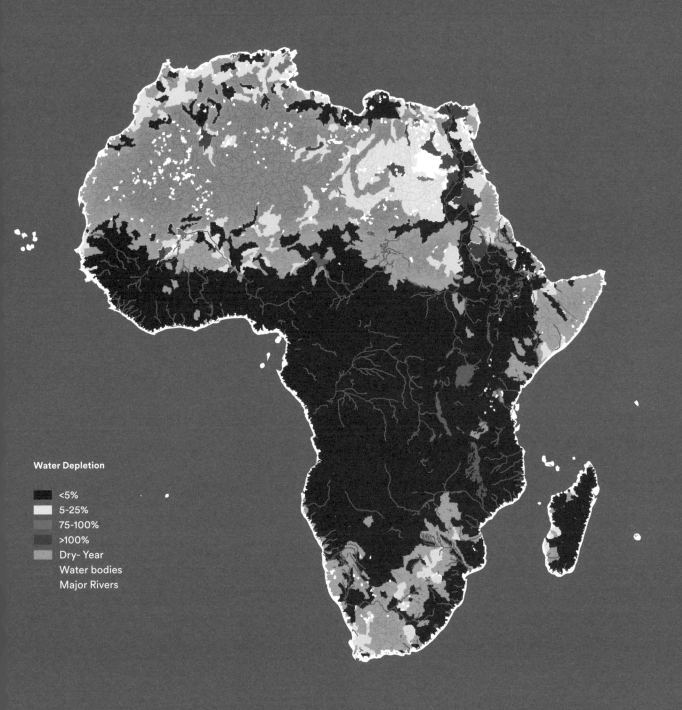

Water Depletion

- <5%
- 5-25%
- 75-100%
- >100%
- Dry- Year
- Water bodies
- Major Rivers

Whilst only a few major river basins exist in northern Africa, and many coastal areas experience physical water scarcity, some of the continent's largest and most saturated aquifers and groundwater systems can be found here.

7 DESIMER FACTORS OF SUSTAINABLE DEVELOPMENT

Title: Dream Chasers-Boys on a Time Capsule | Medium: Photography | Year: 2017 | Artist: Wilfred Ukpong

Demographics
Economics
Socio-politics
Infrastructure
Morphology
Environment
Resources

DESIMER is a research methodology using broad quantitative analysis to unpack human and environmental dynamics that influence developments in any context — particularly in the complex socio-economic and environmental realities of African cities and communities. The collection of data and maps distils information pertaining to seven factors: Demographics, Economics, Socio-politics, Infrastructure, Morphology, Environment, and Resources (referred in this book as the 7 DESIMER factors of sustainable urban development), to create a comprehensive analysis and report of a vast amount of information about issues of urbanization and climate change in African cities and communities. The data is not typically viewed in a visual manner or concurrently, thus by mapping these we provide a unique comparative body of research. This approach also allows city planners, architects and designers to understand the factors that typically exist outside of the realm of design to help make informed decisions about where design and planning can have the most meaningful impact. The results of mapping in this way provide very clear visual and quantitative insights on information and facts on Africa that may have been previously misconstrued or otherwise not readily available.

Furthermore, comparing the maps enables one to clearly identify emerging patterns in indexes or correlations between developmental factors. These guide a multi-disciplinary approach to thinking about development in Africa. Each dataset used in this chapter is from a reputable source such as the World Bank, Global Economy, Our World in Data amongst others, and can be found in the bibliography. The following chapter summarizes findings with key facts cited from the DESIMER factors. These data sets include:

Demographics: Birth rates, population density, city populations, urban population growth
Economics: Economic growth, foreign direct Investment, inflation, GDP per capita
Socio-political: Internal displacement caused by conflict, gender inequality, Covid-19 containment protocols, corruption
Infrastructure: Container port traffic, logistics performance, internet usage, CO_2 emissions from transport
Morphology: City elevation, settlement, electricity usage, rural vs urban settlement
Environment: Annual precipitation, internal displacement caused by flooding, urban exposure to flooding, frequency of floods, storms & wet movements per country
Resources: Agricultural exports, water stress, national forest cover, income from natural resources

In 2014, Kunlé Adeyemi and Suzanne Lettieri initiated the first of two advanced architecture studios titled Water & the City, meant to identify and bridge critical gaps in systems that inhibit healthy development in African cities by water. Initiated at Cornell University, the prompt later became the framework for other studios at Columbia, Harvard and Princeton Universities. In the studios, the filtering of open-source, data-driven information was paired with site visits and on-the-ground interactions with the people living, working and studying in 'African Water Cities', including Dar es Salaam, Abidjan, Durban, and Cabo Verde. This approach intentionally drew out the gaps in information that exist between modalities and also, importantly, debunked preconceived notions commonly held regarding Africa;

for example, incorrect notions of scale, continental generalizations around poverty, or the sentiment that the students could 'fix' a condition rather than learn from it. While the studio situated data mapping as a strategy for urban and architectural conceptual development, it also confronted the augmented power that maps hold. The importance of seeing data through multiple vantage points and bringing awareness to the nuances that get lost in maps then spawned the collection of essays found in this volume that accompany the research.

The following essays are from seven professionals specializing in topics that are framed through the lens of the 7 DESIMER factors, which explore the challenges and opportunities illustrated in the maps and their real-life experiences of the conditions at play.

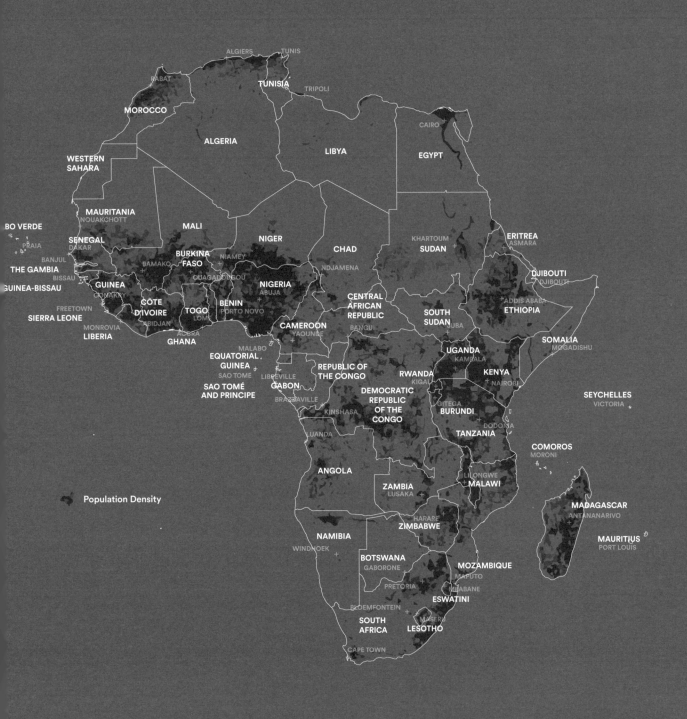

Population Density

African communities and cities are expanding rapidly into unchartered territories.
Africa's population surge, migration and other demographic trends will be a major driver
for the way cities develop.

Demographics

Beach on New Years Day in Durban, South Africa

'Africa may need to build 50 cities the size of Lagos by 2050, to account for more than half of the growth of the world's population projected between 2022 and 2050.'

Makoko, Lagos, 2019

Demographics

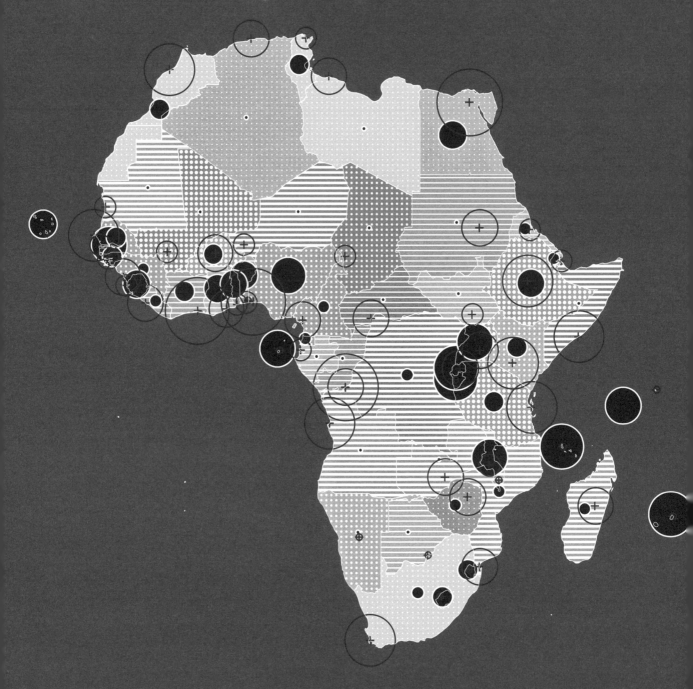

Urban population growth is occurring particularly across Africa's tropics. The highest birth rates in Africa are occurring inland, in the central and western part of the continent whilst the densest countries and most populous cities in Africa are situated along the continent's coastlines.

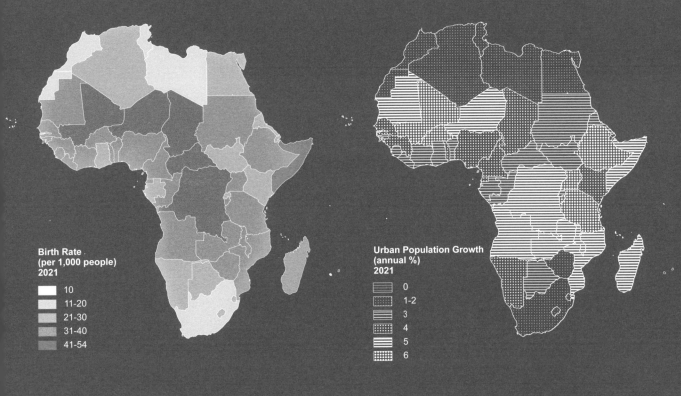

**Birth Rate
(per 1,000 people)
2021**

- 10
- 11-20
- 21-30
- 31-40
- 41-54

**Urban Population Growth
(annual %)
2021**

- 0
- 1-2
- 3
- 4
- 5
- 6

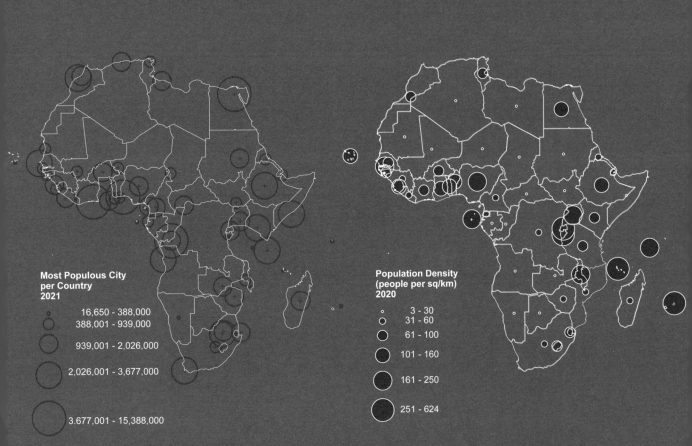

**Most Populous City
per Country
2021**

- 16,650 - 388,000
- 388,001 - 939,000
- 939,001 - 2,026,000
- 2,026,001 - 3,677,000
- 3,677,001 - 15,388,000

**Population Density
(people per sq/km)
2020**

- 3 - 30
- 31 - 60
- 61 - 100
- 101 - 160
- 161 - 250
- 251 - 624

AFRICA. CONTINENT ON THE MOVE, WITHIN ITSELF
Christopher Changwe Nshimbi

Maouloud festival in Mali

Internal, intra- and intercontinental migration define human mobility in Africa. The continent has a long history of migration. And despite popular narratives that Africa is on the move en masse to Europe and high-income countries such as the USA, migration within individual African countries and international migration within the continent prevail over migration to overseas destinations. More migration actually occurs between proximate countries and within the major regions of Africa such as the Southern African Development Community (SADC) or the Economic Community of West African States (ECOWAS) than towards destinations outside the continent[1]. The large rural and youthful population in many African countries coupled with rapid urbanization make rural-urban migration prominent along with other diverse patterns within respective African countries and internationally between the countries. Circulations between proximate countries and within Africa's major regions form distinctive patterns of mobility on the continent. These dynamics not only redefine local, national, regional and continental landscapes in Africa but also indicate the socioeconomic value and cultural significance of migration.

Demographic Makeup of the Continent

Discussion of the demographic constitution of Africa should consider the variety, diversity, dynamism and vastness of the continent. Africa comprises ethnically diverse countries. These vary in size and nature. Large countries such as the Democratic Republic of the Congo (DRC), Ethiopia and Nigeria have individual populations that range from about 100 million to over 200 million people, while small countries such as the Comoros, Cape Verde, Djibouti and the Seychelles have less than one million people each. Africa also includes island states, states on the mainland and some completely landlocked countries on the mainland. The total population of Africa in 2022 accounted for almost 17 per cent of total global population, having grown from about 9 per cent in 1950 and 14 per cent in 2005. This means that the continent has had the fastest growing population in the world since the 1980s. Projections by the United Nations Department of Economic and Social Affairs[2] show that Africa's population will double between 2022 and 2050 and surpass two billion people by the late 2040s. More than half of the world's total population growth during this period will again occur in Africa alone.

The growth in Africa's population is partly due to typically high average fertility rates. At three births per woman, Africa's fertility makes it the continent with the highest annual population growth rate in the world. Continentally, fertility slightly rose up to about 7 children per woman in the 1950s until the early 1970s and then significantly diverged among the major regions of Africa thereafter. In Southern Africa, for instance, it fell to 2.71 children per woman in 2015 from four children per woman in the 1980s and six children per woman in the 1960s. Compare

this with Central Africa, where it continued rising from the 1950s level of six children per woman to 6.76 in the 1980s-1990s. It then slowly fell to a still high six children per woman in the period 2010-2015.

The total population of Africa in 2022 accounted for almost 17 per cent of total global population, having grown from about 9 per cent in 1950 and 14 per cent in 2005.

This growth is, however, not homogenous across the continent or its regions. Variations exist at the country level too. The DRC and Nigeria have stable but still very high fertility while in countries such as Ethiopia, Malawi and Kenya fertility is rapidly declining. Also, countries such as the DRC, Mali and Somalia have very high fertility rates that exceed six children per woman. This all translates into annual growth rates of population for individual African countries that range from 0.5 per cent to four per cent a year.

Africa's growing population is also due to declining mortality. Life expectancy on the continent rose from less than 40 years in the 1950s to about 56 years in 2019[3]. But variations between Africa's major regions and individual countries exist here too. In ECOWAS, for example, life expectancy is slightly above 55 years and that of individual countries within the region, like Nigeria, slightly above 50 years. A combination of factors contributes to the noteworthy decline in mortality witnessed in Africa since the 1950s and 1960s. A major contributor is the decline in infant mortality, which dropped by almost 30 per cent in the period between 2000-2005 and 2010-2015 for Africa as a whole. Most noticeable rates of decline in this regard included, among others, 41 per cent in Ethiopia, 43 per cent in the Congo, 46 per cent in Botswana and 51 per cent in Rwanda. Improved public health from concerted fight against tropical diseases, and better nutrition and sanitation contribute to a healthier Africa, where people live longer. The cited trends paint a picture of a demographically dynamic Africa.

> Additionally, a variety of other socioeconomic and structural factors such as climate, size and density, economic cycles and income levels, environmental disasters and war and conflict, among others, influence urban dynamics.

The 'Africa Urbanizing' Question

Africa is experiencing a rapid urban transition with about 49 per cent of its population projected to be urban by 2035, up from 31 per cent in 1990. The continent's urban population will probably triple to 1.33 billion by 2050 and, together with Asia, account for almost 90 per cent of the global urban population[4]. However, Africa follows a unique urbanization trajectory not based on, for example, improvements in agricultural productivity that lead to the restructuring of economies into manufacturing and services, as development theory and experience in other parts of the world show. Many African countries are urbanizing despite declining industrial output, for instance. The different regions and countries of Africa exhibit varying urbanization trends too. The urban population in least urbanized African countries such as Eritrea, Rwanda, Burkina Faso and Lesotho manifests the highest annual rate of growth when compared with countries such as the Congo, Djibouti, Gabon and South Africa, which are more urbanized. Urbanization in the latter group of countries tends to result from natural population increases and not from rural-urban migration, which largely contributes to urbanization in the former group of countries. Urban-rural disparities related to basic social service are high in the countries with the highest rates of urbanization. Hence, economic and social opportunities in urban areas constitute pull factors, making migration an important part of population growth.

Among the top most populous cities in Africa, cities such as Lagos (Africa's largest) in Nigeria, Kinshasa (Africa's second largest) in the DRC, among several others, are positioned near water bodies. While the location and growth of such cities can historically be linked to colonial and immediate post-independence times, environmental constraints such as water availability constitute key influences on both urban form and growth as the cities of Lagos and Kinshasa show.

Causes for Urbanization

Besides fertility and mortality, migration is one of the factors that make up projected changes in population. Additionally, a variety of other socioeconomic and structural factors such as climate, size and density, economic cycles and income levels, environmental disasters and war and conflict, among others, influence urban dynamics. The factors may not have equal and/or uniform impact on urbanization but some of them are more important contributors, especially at lower stages of urbanization.[5] In the case of Africa, high population growth and contribution to natural increase in populations in urban areas is highlighted as a major driver of urbanization since the 1990s. However, state and local government institutions as well as the national context play significant roles in urbanization. Where states reclassify rural settlements that grow beyond urban population sizes, this also contributes to urbanization. In such cases, political influences are greatest in shaping urban phenomena and several African countries and cities manifest such impact of urban policies and planning.

A Future Outlook

Africa is experiencing an exponential growth in population alongside urbanization. The scale and rate of urbanization on the continent is certainly reshaping its demographic profile and socioeconomic and environmental outcomes. The projected tripling of the urban population in Africa will greatly stress economic, political, societal and physical infrastructure in the continent's cities and megacities. This provides both opportunities and challenges for the continent. On the positive side, urbanization can be harnessed for structural transformation and economic growth. Stakeholders can, for instance, consider the nexus between urban development and industrial development through carefully crafted strategies, policies and investments aimed at making cities sustainable.

The projected tripling of the urban population in Africa will greatly stress economic, political, societal and physical infrastructure in the continent's cities and megacities.

HELICE

Back from fishing, Bonny Island, Nigeria, 2006

'Sub-Saharan Africa has the highest rate of adult population involved in early-stage entrepreneurial activity.'

People waiting for the fishing boats to come into the harbor, Elmina, Central Region, Ghana

Economics

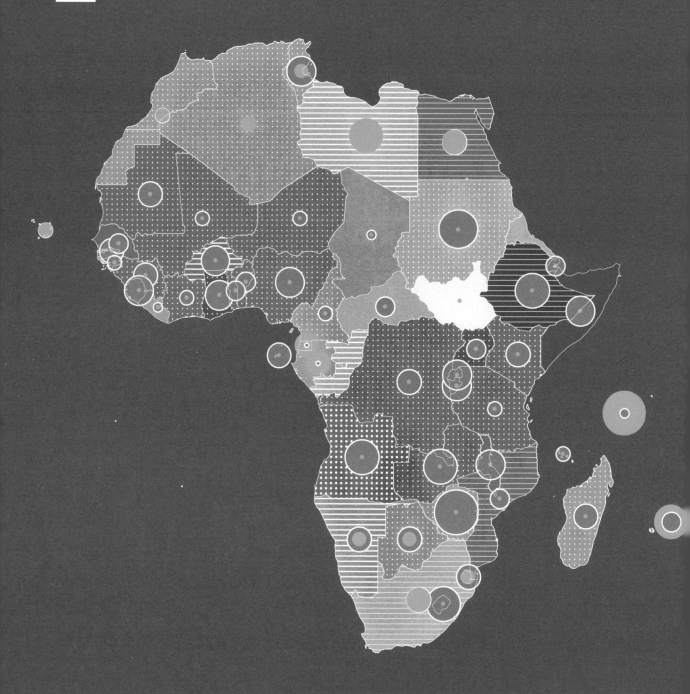

With the exception of South Sudan, economic growth is occurring throughout the continent. Mostly in west, central and east Africa. Across the continent, Net FDI is mostly negative, with some exceptions. Some northern, southern African and island nations have the largest GDP per capita whilst inflation remains high across the continent.

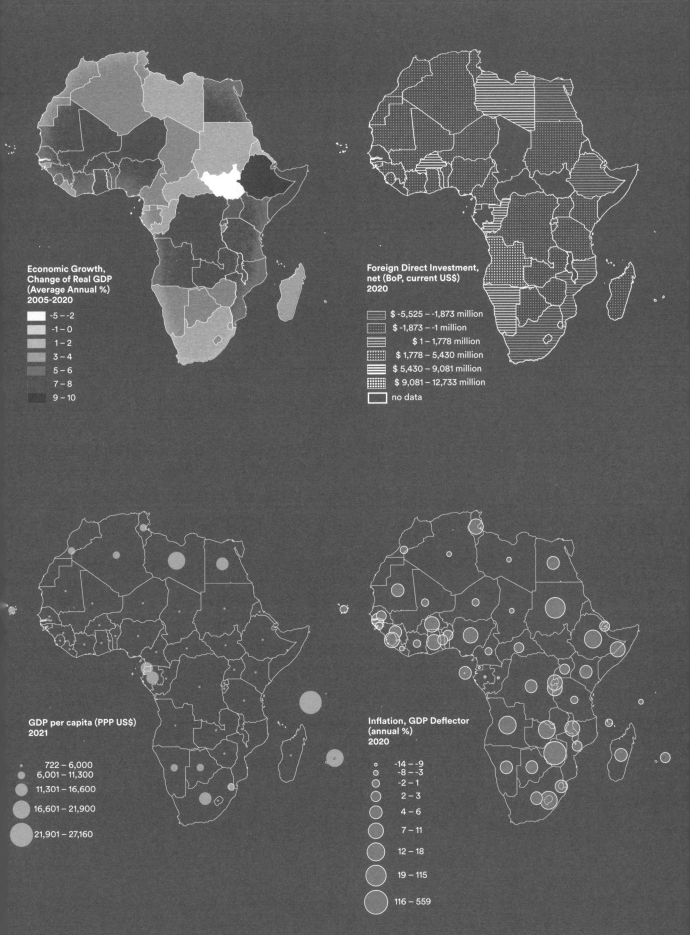

**Economic Growth,
Change of Real GDP
(Average Annual %)
2005-2020**

- -5 – -2
- -1 – 0
- 1 – 2
- 3 – 4
- 5 – 6
- 7 – 8
- 9 – 10

**Foreign Direct Investment,
net (BoP, current US$)
2020**

- $ -5,525 – -1,873 million
- $ -1,873 – -1 million
- $ 1 – 1,778 million
- $ 1,778 – 5,430 million
- $ 5,430 – 9,081 million
- $ 9,081 – 12,733 million
- no data

**GDP per capita (PPP US$)
2021**

- 722 – 6,000
- 6,001 – 11,300
- 11,301 – 16,600
- 16,601 – 21,900
- 21,901 – 27,160

**Inflation, GDP Deflector
(annual %)
2020**

- -14 – -9
- -8 – -3
- -2 – -1
- 2 – 3
- 4 – 6
- 7 – 11
- 12 – 18
- 19 – 115
- 116 – 559

GROWING WITH THE TIDE
Joy Antonia Kategekwa

Large container vessel passing the New Suez Canal near Ismailia, Egypt, 2017

How are cities and communities situated by water bodies growing whilst adapting to the impacts of climate change? And what is the appropriate development response for managing the intersection between water cities and climate change? This essay debates these issues commencing by situating the overall economic context within which Africa's water cities evolve, taking into account the impact of recent global shocks. It looks at how the effects of sea level rise, increased rainfall, flooding and droughts resulting from climate change impact economic development in Africa, and finally, shares reflections on solutions for more sustainable futures for Africa's water cities and their people.

Africa's Economic Growth Prospects

We live in uncertain times. Recent shocks, from pandemics to the war in Ukraine, shook the core of nations and societies, unleashing a global regression in human development for the second year in a row.[1] In 2021, sub-Saharan Africa experienced negative growth at -2.1 per cent .[2] African countries struggle with high inflation, rising food and energy prices and public debt.[3] According to the World Bank, in 2021 Ghana already had a ten per cent inflation rate[4], and by July 2022, this had risen to 31.7 per cent (an 18-year high).[5] Prospects remain weak—with Africa projected to grow at four per cent in 2023[6]—far below the required seven to ten per cent to meet the global sustainable development goals.

People living in Africa's water cities were severely hit by these seismic shocks. The Covid-19 pandemic broke global supply chains, halting commercial activities of shipping lines, and yet they are the major economic booster for coastal cities. This cost communities their livelihoods. Almost entirely.

On its part, the war in Ukraine exposed Africa's over-reliance on external food systems for grain and fertilizer, and the resulting imported inflation unleashed a still transmitting cost-of- living crisis, ravaging economies across the board, but especially so in water cities, which depend on international trade for their survival. The windfall of high prices of food, fuel and fertilizer could not be cashed in by water city dwellers for two main reasons. One: most shipping lines and associated enterprises are foreign-owned[7] and two: water city dwellers would still need to meet the same high costs in the price of bread, fuel, and other basic services.

The polycrisis Africa witnesses demonstrates the urgency to invest in resilience. And water cities will play a key role in this, since they are the fulcrum of global connectivity.

Climate Change Rocks Africa's Water Cities – Sets Back its Development

Water cities will continue to play a critical role in accelerating Africa's development. Home to some of the mega ports driving trade internationally, cities such as Durban, Mombasa, Djibouti, Accra and Lagos have the potential to catalyse Africa's growth and transformation.

The water cities of advanced economies had the opportunity to grow in the pre-climate change era, but today, the climate emergency demands new standards and a deeper sensitivity to, and harmony between, growth and industrial policy on the one hand and nature's wellness on the other.[8] For this reason, the relationship between prosperity, people and planet is at the heart of the global sustainable development goals.[9]

> Home to some of the mega ports driving trade internationally, cities such as Durban, Mombasa, Djibouti, Accra and Lagos have the potential to catalyse Africa's growth and transformation.

While the impact of climate change is felt across all of Africa, it is uniquely grave in cities next to coasts, rivers, lagoons, and lakes. According to the World Meteorological Organization, 'Africa's climate has warmed more than the global average since pre-industrial times (1850-1900). In parallel, the sea level rise along African coastlines is faster than the global mean, contributing to increases in the frequency and severity of coastal flooding and erosion, and salinity in low-lying cities.'[10] The 2022 floods in Nigeria reminded us that adaptation and mitigation are not policy options of theoretical value. They are tools for survival. Oguntola quotes the Federal Government of Nigeria as reporting that these floods displaced over 1.4 million people, killed over 603 people, and injured more than 2,400 persons, damaging 82,035 houses and 332,327 hectares of land.[11] And Nigeria is not even unique.[12]

Even amidst the climate change tide, Africa's water cities continue to attract large populations from rural areas with greener pastures who place their hope in the blue economy of water cities. This wave of rural urban migration is largely youth-driven. They come looking for prospects in lucrative services markets such as shipping and logistics, or economic activities such as fishing.

But there is also the phenomenon of climate-induced urban-rural human mobility in Africa. According to the Africa Climate Mobility Initiative, 122,000 people are expected to move out of Dar es Salaam alone, because of the climate emergency.[13] Participants in this climate-induced mobility will likely end up in rural areas, which as we have seen above are themselves ill-equipped to fulfil the dreams of young people. This rural-urban-urban-rural conundrum creates a vicious cycle of need, complex social interactions and exacerbates social tension.

Africa Climate Mobility Report[14]
In the Sahel, climate change explains the growing disappearance of Lake Chad, a situation that causes conflict over scarce resources, impacting livelihoods and ecosystems of herder communities. The region is experiencing increasing temperatures and more frequent weather extremes are anticipated for the time to come—'hitting harder than other parts of the world.'[15]

Solutions for Water Cities to Grow with the Tide Amidst an Uncertain Future
Africa must invest in adaptation. But it requires innovative approaches to creating and accessing financing, including from the dividends of well-managed natural resources that the continent has in abundance. This is why tackling illicit financial flows is urgent.

Seizing opportunities in the African Continental Free Trade Area (AfCFTA) prospects in shipping and ports-related services (such as transport and logistics) provides hope for Africa's coastal cities to position themselves as connectors for intra-African trade. Success for water cities will depend on deliberate actions to increase transaction volumes in intra-African trade. This in turn requires investments in the infrastructure of connectivity through implementing plans like the African Union's Programme for Infrastructure Development of Africa (PIDA).[16]

Acting on economic diversification will reduce water cities' reliance on vulnerable sectors, offering them a more balanced menu of options to absorb shocks in one sector with activity in another. This is why investing in agriculture, manufacturing and the knowledge economy is key.

Expanding and building new cities across Africa's hinterland to take advantage of the 60 per cent of the world's unutilized arable land will pull people into jobs in agriculture and the industries springing therefrom. Targeting such hinterland city expansion to areas where Africa's raw materials are, will create benefits for rural communities. For example, Ghana's shea butter growing communities in Tamale could benefit from a new city, as would Kenya's tea producing Kericho region, or Tanzania's tanzanite mining Moshi region. If these cities have amenities such as schools and health centres, people will move there, creating more opportunities for those employed in water cities. The youth can play a role in building these cities—inceasing incomes and overall production—which will work well in shoring Africa out of the economic recession.

Climate-induced mobility requires urgent attention to create safe and orderly migration. There is a need to promote full ratification of the African Union Protocol on the Free Movement of Persons to facilitate this.

Recent global shocks have put the unique vulnerability of water cities in sharp focus because of their exposure to climate change and international trade shocks. Solutions ultimately lie in a new development approach that prioritizes building resilience. COP 27 gave some hope with the decision to establish a loss and damage facility to cover development gains wiped off in Africa and other developing countries. Now we must get to its implementation.

> Africa must invest in adaptation. But it requires innovative approaches to creating and accessing financing, including from the dividends of well-managed natural resources that the continent has in abundance.

Safaricom's M-Pesa service in Nairobi, Kenya

Socio-politics

Waterfront in Cotonou, Benin

'The first settlers of Venice called 'incolae lacunae' were lagoon dwellers – quite like the people of Makoko, Lagos.'

Makoko, Lagos

Socio-politics

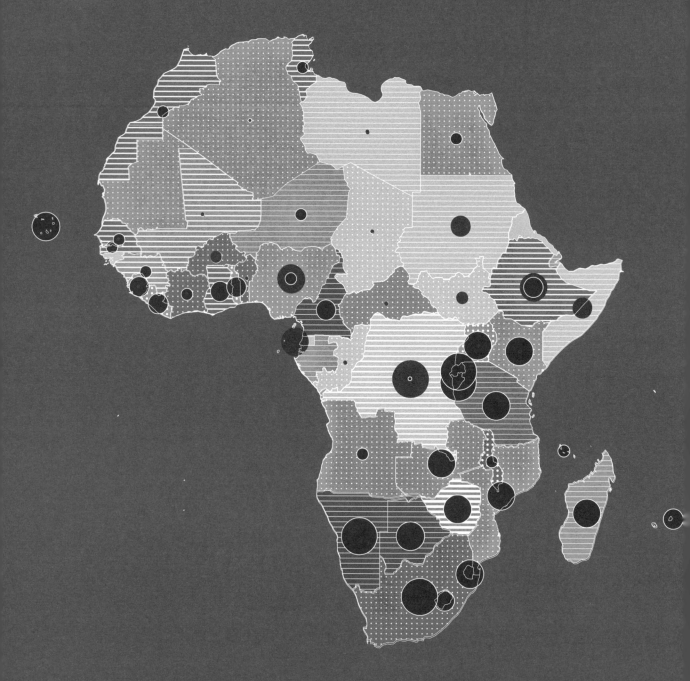

Across the continent, gender equality is most positively experienced in countries with the lowest levels of perceived corruption. Internal displacement caused by conflict occurs most heavily in eastern and central Africa whilst levels of Covid-19 containment restrictions vary throughout.

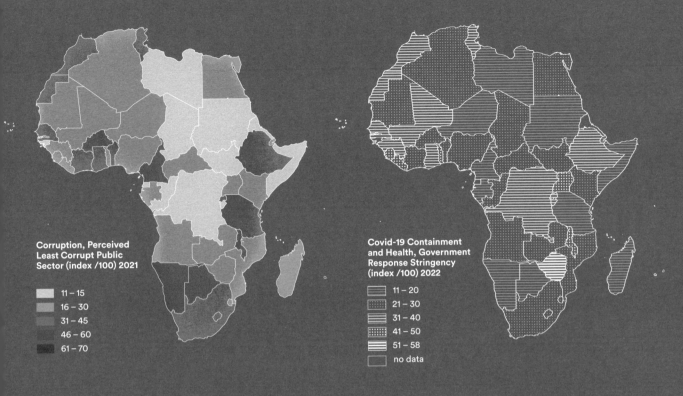

**Corruption, Perceived
Least Corrupt Public
Sector (index /100) 2021**

- 11 – 15
- 16 – 30
- 31 – 45
- 46 – 60
- 61 – 70

**Covid-19 Containment
and Health, Government
Response Stringency
(index /100) 2022**

- 11 – 20
- 21 – 30
- 31 – 40
- 41 – 50
- 51 – 58
- no data

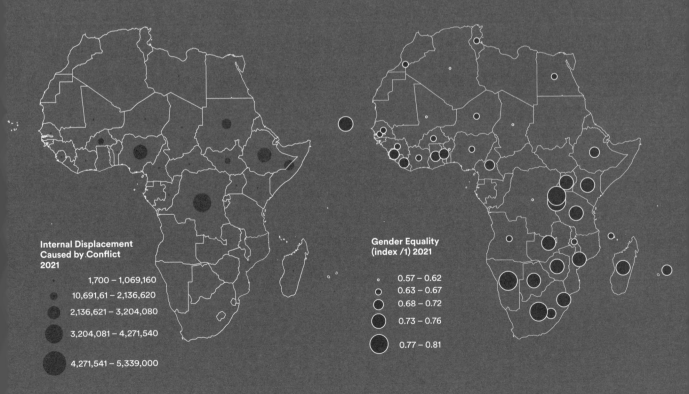

**Internal Displacement
Caused by Conflict
2021**

- 1,700 – 1,069,160
- 10,691,61 – 2,136,620
- 2,136,621 – 3,204,080
- 3,204,081 – 4,271,540
- 4,271,541 – 5,339,000

**Gender Equality
(index /1) 2021**

- 0.57 – 0.62
- 0.63 – 0.67
- 0.68 – 0.72
- 0.73 – 0.76
- 0.77 – 0.81

SOCIO-POLITICS OF URBANIZATION: A VIEW FROM LAGOS
Taibat Lawanson

Creek at Victoria Island, Lagos, Nigeria

Africa is home to the most rapidly urbanizing cities in the world with three megacities – Cairo, Kinshasa and Lagos, and cities such as Dar es Salaam, Nairobi, Luanda and Khartoum almost at megacity status. However, Africa's urbanization is typified by the urbanization of poverty. This has given rise to intense socio-economic disparities and increased socio-political complexities.

The continent is unable to effectively respond to the negative impacts of climate change, and urban access reveals glaring inequalities across gender, demography and socio-economic dimensions. In 2021, women in countries such as Nigeria, Chad, Congo and Niger with gender inequality rates of between 0.6 and 0.7 suffered disproportionately from challenges related to income, health, political participation and discrimination. Across Africa, contestations for resources often result in conflict. In fact, in 2021 alone, over 11 million people were displaced due to natural disasters and conflicts.

In many African cities, water is both a blessing and a curse. A blessing because of the immense opportunities for navigation, access to resources and trade partners; and a curse because of the socio-economic and environmental hazards that have become more intense due to climate change, anthropogenic activities, and globalization. Coupled with widespread corruption that further exacerbates these vulnerabilities, rather than enjoying the urban advantage, the average African urban resident is suffering the urban penalty.

A predominant number of Lagos slum communities are located on or close to water and are at constant threat of evictions due to increasing elite interest in waterfront locations based on perceived value.

Elite Land Capture and the Allure of the Waterfront

Lagos, Nigeria, is popularly known as 'Africa's Water City', a status earned from its natural water endowment which acts as a valuable resource for fishing, port gateway and water-based livelihoods. Water bodies and wetlands cover over forty percent of the total land area of Lagos. With a population in excess of 20 million and its strategic position as Nigeria's economic and industrial hub, its low-lying status makes it vulnerable to flooding. Residents of Lagos are faced with increasingly severe annual flooding, which is made worse by sea level rising and land sinking.

Clear gaps in providing appropriate water infrastructure continually pose a challenge in the city. Effective waterway management is constrained due to perennial jurisdictional and operational tussles between the Lagos State Waterways Regulatory Authority (LASWA) and National Inland Waterways Authority (NIWA), while activities of the Lagos state Ministry of Waterfront Infrastructure management often clash with those of the ministries of environment, physical planning and urban development and even transportation.

Over the years, the city has embarked on a number of water-related megaprojects to actualize its vision to be 'Africa's model megacity'. An example is the Eko Atlantic City, which is meant to address climate change challenges and catalyse economic development simultaneously. Though laudable, what is emerging from these ambitious efforts at coastal regeneration is socio-spatial segregation and enclaving, which further embeds the serious socio-economic inequalities that Lagos manifests.

Lagos is characterized by sharp inequality, with both widespread poverty and substantial wealth. A predominant number of Lagos slum communities are located on or close to water and are at constant threat of evictions due to increasing elite interest in waterfront locations based on perceived value. Over the years, slum communities such as Maroko and Otodogbame have been completely annihilated and replaced with luxury real estate. Others such as Badia and Ilubinrin have experienced eviction after eviction, which has resulted in gentrification.

We have also seen a wave of government endorsed self-made islands such as Eko Atlantic City, Banana Island and the proposed Orange Island and Ocean city, which are being developed and marketed as smart cities offering technology, luxury and functionality. The eco-tourism narrative is also being adopted in the commercialization of beaches and the conversion of hitherto environmentally unspoiled communities along the Lagos Lagoon to luxury resorts and playgrounds of the ultra-wealthy. Unfortunately, these land reclamation actions require extensive sand dredging, which inadvertently exacerbates flood vulnerability across the entire city.

Responding to Climate Vulnerability

Even though Lagos is vulnerable to flooding practically everywhere, addressing the effects of flood vulnerability has socio-economic dimensions. While hard infrastructure is being deployed through public funds to protect high-income areas in the Victoria Island and Lekki axis, affected low-income communities in Alimosho, Ikorodu and Bariga often have to resort to self-help, thus debunking the myth that the urban poor are irresponsible custodians of their communities. Leading up to the rainy season (April – October), community development associations across Lagos can be seen mobilizing funds and in-kind contributions for the construction and/or clearance of drainages, the purchase and installation of sandbags to aid mobility, and in serious cases, making preparations for temporary relocation should the floods become unbearable.

Interestingly, many slum communities consider the flood situation as a seasonal inconvenience they have learnt to cope with. Out of 1682 responses by the Lagos State Emergency Response Agencies, only three were flood related. For the urban poor, access to educational and economic opportunities is a more existential challenge, and women play a prominent role in ensuring that children are able to overcome challenges of access.

Desertification and climate induced drought is also triggering conflict-induced migration of internally displaced persons (IDP) from rural farming communities in Nigeria's northern region to urban areas in the South. Lagos is estimated to host the highest number of independent IDP migrants in Nigeria. This new wave of IDP migration to Lagos, and their attempts at urban integration is resulting in new spatial forms including shack settlements in the city peri-urban axis and urban acupuncture in the form of emerging farming settlements on small pockets of land around the city's core. Furthermore, those who attempt to infiltrate existing slums face stigmatization and harassment, which sometimes degenerates into ethnic clashes and contestations for urban resources.

A 'Climate-resilient' Urban Future: Top-down and Bottom-up Approaches Are Required

Lagos state government has been proactive in policy development for climate change mitigation and adaptation. The Lagos Resilience Strategy and Climate Action Plan are indicative of this. However, these important policy interventions have been largely driven by external stimuli — C40 in the case of Climate Action Plan and 100 Resilient Cities (now Global Resilient Cities Network); and are yet to be effectively mainstreamed into everyday urban processes. In fact, there has been more focus on the larger-scale heavy investmentdriven approaches to the neglect of smaller-scale quick wins. For example, there is low uptake of domestic waste sorting, backyard gardening, and active travel, which promote circular economy, mitigate food insecurity and improve air quality at micro-levels. Interestingly, we also find that women play an active role in these micro-scale activities.

In responding to climate vulnerability and associated challenges of urban life, there is a need to learn from and scale up the granular activities of residents of flood prone areas in Lagos. For example, the agrarian skills that IDPs bring with them can be an opportunity for scaling up urban agriculture in Lagos, which is a key initiative in both the Climate Action Plan and resilience strategy. Community agency such as Ajegunle Ikorodu's Community Resilience Action plan, which has been used to successfully negotiate improved public service delivery and Irede's Creek City urban redevelopment project, which led to government and civil society collaboration for an Affordable Housing trust fund, provide an opportunity to catalyse community led activities for emergency preparedness and early warning systems for health- and climate-related incidents.

The future of Lagos and many other African water cities threatened by climate change lies in actively working on both top-down and bottom-up strategies aimed at reducing socioeconomic inequities and environmental vulnerabilities, reforming water sector governance, and leaning on the ingrained resilience attributes of local communities.

> In responding to climate vulnerability and associated challenges of urban life, there is a need to learn from and scale up the granular activities of residents of flood prone areas in Lagos.

Members of waterfront communities in Lagos in a flotilla to commemorate one year of the forceful eviction of Otodo Gbame

Infrastructure

Jetty close to Ganvie, Benin

'Multilateralism is the key to realizing the crucial infrastructure required for coastal adaptation and economic growth.'

Oko-baba Sawmill, Lagos, Nigeria

Infrastructure

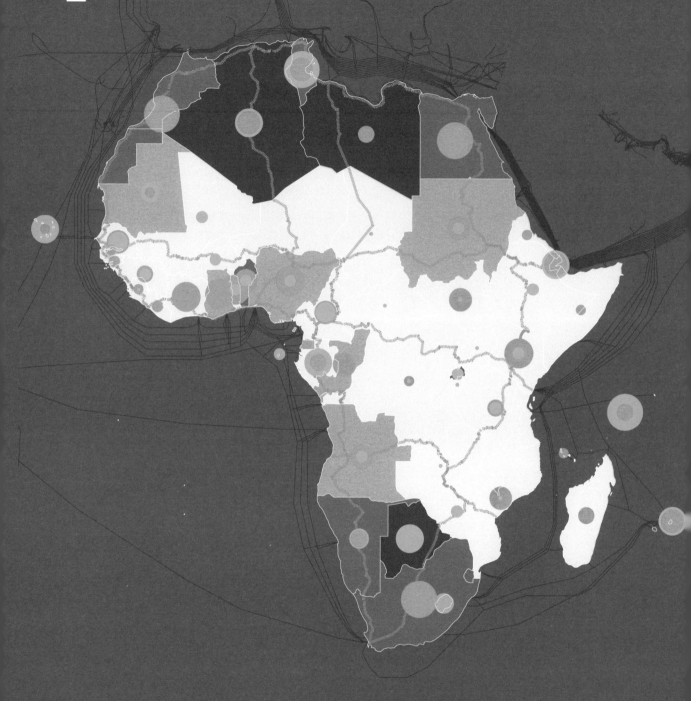

Per Capita, CO$_2$ emissions from road, rail and pipeline transport are particularly high in northern and southern Africa. Container port traffic is also highest here. Countries along the coast have the highest internet usage.

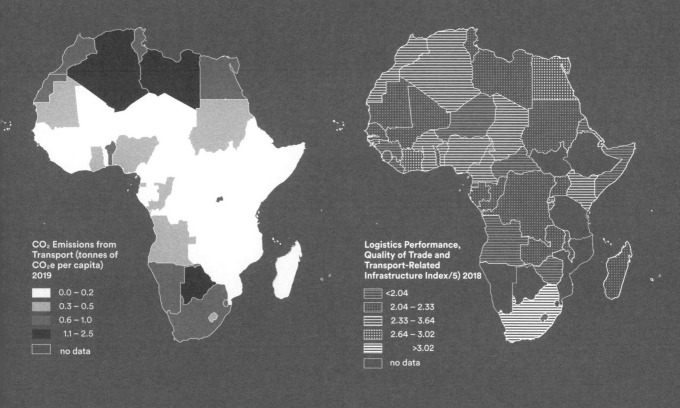

CO₂ Emissions from Transport (tonnes of CO₂e per capita) 2019

- 0.0 – 0.2
- 0.3 – 0.5
- 0.6 – 1.0
- 1.1 – 2.5
- no data

Logistics Performance, Quality of Trade and Transport-Related Infrastructure Index/5) 2018

- <2.04
- 2.04 – 2.33
- 2.33 – 3.64
- 2.64 – 3.02
- >3.02
- no data

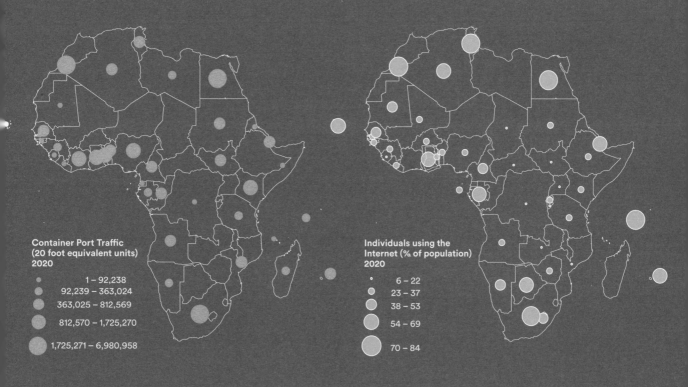

Container Port Traffic (20 foot equivalent units) 2020

- 1 – 92,238
- 92,239 – 363,024
- 363,025 – 812,569
- 812,570 – 1,725,270
- 1,725,271 – 6,980,958

Individuals using the Internet (% of population) 2020

- 6 – 22
- 23 – 37
- 38 – 53
- 54 – 69
- 70 – 84

COASTAL INFRASTRUCTURE IN WEST AFRICA
Denis W. Aheto & Peter Kristensen

Concrete breakwater at the Port of Alexandria, Egypt, 2018

West Africa's coastal zone is productive, biodiversity-rich, and critical for the region's economy. Yet, it is subject to ongoing severe environmental degradation, mainly from coastal erosion, flooding, and pollution. Erosion of the West African coast is triggered by poorly managed coastal infrastructure altering coastal sediment transport, such as deep-water ports, with limited planning and consideration of its impacts. Large transversal river barriers like hydropower dams, also play an important role as they can alter fluvial sediment transport and lead to coastal unbalances. Cross-border management of coastal sediment, taking a 'sediment budget' approach whereby inbound and existing sediment is modeled, will eventually be imperative to manage the coastline in West Africa. Commercial sand winning activities, pollution from plastics, and illegal artisanal gold mining impact human health, livelihoods and coastal ecosystem services. Climate change and variability in particular affects the people and resources as seen with intermittent floods, severe drought, and increasing air and water temperatures. Many activities, such as sand winning, fishery overexploitation, and infrastructural development in coastal areas are exacerbated by climate change effects and natural hazards. The intensity of these stressors is likely to increase in the future. Unfortunately, national activities currently do not give sufficient priority to climate change issues.

The Rationale for International Partnerships

From 2015, the World Bank engaged with countries on the challenge to address coastal erosion in West Africa. The phenomenon of coastal erosion in the region was well known by the governments and the scientific community. While solutions exist, the efforts to manage the challenge did not sufficiently prevent coastal communities from losing their homes and lands to coastal erosion. Because of the complexity of the challenge, the World Bank also engaged regional institutions, international partners, the private sector, and the higher education community. While the World Bank itself can provide finance where government requests exist, many more pieces are needed to develop and act on solutions.

Why is the Coast so Difficult to Manage?

Following a period of unbundling the problem, the World Bank found that four main reasons why coastline had been so difficult to manage: First, solutions are complex because they require data modeling to find the right solutions to resist the powerful wave energy that permanently pounds the coast. Second, interventions are costly, especially when hard solutions for sea defense are required, and public financing is scarce. Private sector finance is not readily suitable for coastal protection as there is no revenue generation from the investment, although this does not mean that the private sector has no role (more about this later). Third, multiple sectors ministries are needed to manage the coastline, including those responsible for land

management, fisheries, urban, energy, and ports. Third, the technical solutions are complex as they in many cases require cross-border collaboration, and working at local, national and international levels. Finally, it is evident that all of this requires a long-term commitment, also at the political level to actively manage the coast.

Studying a time series of coastlines following placement of infrastructure on the coast, and following loss of natural habitat that helps retain coastal sediment, it became clear that a holistic approach to coastal zone development was needed. And what about climate change? We know that sea level rise may be in the order of 30 cm by 2050, and precipitation could increase by 13 per cent (WACA climate report). However, relatively, one can plausibly conclude that compared to coastal erosion caused by obstructing coastal infrastructure, climate change may not be the dominating factor for loss of sediment and land in coastal areas. Nevertheless, given the prospects of extreme weather events combining storm surge, lunar high tide, and sea-level rise, a single event causing extreme erosion should not be a surprise. The residual development challenge is clear: how can coastal countries in West Africa manage their blue economy and coastline, while adapting to climate change?

Economics and the Multiple Challenges

Environmental degradation is costly—to individuals, to societies, and to the environment. In West Africa, coastal degradation takes an important toll on people's health and quality of life. From Mauritania to Gabon, millions of people on the coast suffer from severe erosion, flooding and pollution. These take away lands, homes and lives. Climate change and variability, characterized by rising sea levels and more frequent and violent storms, are exacerbating their predicaments.

Beyond the shattered lives, the harsh consequences of erosion, pollution and flooding are very costly to Benin, Côte d'Ivoire, Senegal and Togo. A new World Bank study reveals in economic terms the cost of the damage in these four countries. Titled The Cost of Coastal Zone Degradation in West Africa[1] the study shows staggering numbers. In 2017 alone, flooding, erosion, and pollution cost about $3.8 billion, or 5.3 per cent of the four countries' GDP. Moreover, coastal degradation causes more than 13,000 deaths a year, primarily due to floods, air and water pollution. In Cote d'Ivoire where floods are most damaging, the cost of degradation was estimated at nearly $2 billion equivalent to 4.9 per cent of its GDP.[2] In Benin, a country prone to erosion, this cost was estimated at $229 million equivalent to 2.5 per cent of the country's GDP. These threats are aggravated by climate change which increases the vulnerability of the coastal communities. These communities are fully affected by flooding due to extreme local rainfall and to rivers overtopping their banks and leading to major damage to assets, houses and infrastructure. Critical ecosystems such as beaches and mangroves as well as many farmlands have been devastated.

Globally, the shocks most frequently reported are natural hazards, especially floods. Immediate impacts of flooding include loss or damage to property, loss of human life, destruction of crops, and deterioration of health conditions owing to waterborne diseases. As communication links and infrastructure such as power plants, roads and bridges are damaged and disrupted, some economic activities may come to a standstill, people are forced to leave their homes and normal life is disrupted. Coastal low-lying areas are prone to natural flooding. Coastal flood-prone areas are dynamic, as daily erosion and accretion affect the contours of the coast, which are exacerbated by human activities through land use and land cover. West African countries are severely affected by floods. Flood frequency has increased in the past 50 years and is expected to increase in the future.[3]

The degradation of water resources on coastal zones is often due to human activities—e.g. poor water and sanitation service provision, mining, tourism, agriculture— and natural factors—e.g. sea level rise leading to salt water intrusion in groundwater. This degradation affects both water quality and quantity, with impacts on people's health and the services provided by ecosystems.

The continent's most vulnerable coastal communities and the fragile marine and coastal ecosystems will need climate adaptation action at scale to prepare for the climate impacts of today and tomorrow.

The WACA Programme
The West Africa Coastal Areas (WACA) Management Program, launched in November 2018, was developed in partnership with West African countries. The program supports regional institutions and countries' efforts to improve the management of their shared coastal resources and reduce the natural and man-made risks affecting coastal communities. The WACA Regional Support Office for the Implementation of Coastal Resilience Investment Projects in West Africa (ResIP1) project has supported interventions in several countries, including: Mauritania, where the ResIP1 project is financing the reinforcement of coastal dunes protecting Nouakchott through biological and mechanical fixation, as well as the filling of priority breaches. The dune of Nouakchott is the capital city's main protection against marine submersion. Most of the city is between 0 m and 4 m above mean sea level, and any overtopping of the dunes by the sea would result in entire districts being flooded. Benin and Togo, where the ResIP1 project is financing the construction of coastal erosion protection measures in the transboundary site between Agbodrafo and Grand-Popo, which is strongly affected by flooding and coastal erosion. The protection measures used include the building of groynes (shore-protection structures built perpendicularly to the shoreline) and a large-scale beach nourishment operation inspired by the Dutch sand motor. Restoration interventions such as lagoon dredging, riverbank stabilization, and revegetation of riverbanks are also being undertaken in the lower Mono river basin to increase community resilience to flooding and erosion.

Sustainable Ports' Partnership
Recognizing that port infrastructure being one of the key coastal infrastructures that must remain sustainable, the Port Management Association of

West and Central Africa (PMAWCA), with support from the WACA Program, explored an innovative approach for West and Central African ports to find common ground, share knowledge, and identify mutually beneficial solutions addressing environmental and social issues in port development and operations. Under the partnership, coastal communities, regional institutions, and global partners will bring expertise and know-how to improve ports' environmental and social performance. The Sustainable Ports' Partnership (SPP) was born.

The SPP is connecting regional partners and global expertise and bring this combination to bear on the task of improving port sustainability. Regional collaboration with strong knowledge partners such as Marine Technology Cooperation Center (MTCC) Africa and Africa's ports community will build the foundation for an innovative south-to-south approach to address the shared environmental and social issues. A key partner in the implementation of the SPP is the Ports Environmental Network – Africa (PENAf)[4] with expertise in sustainability and well-established connections with ports in West and Central Africa which will help to solidify the regional integration of the partnership. Bringing global expertise to the table such as EcoPorts[5] or Green Marine[6] will allow best practices to be integrated into the design and framework of the partnership.

The complex challenges and risks—and the enormous development and livelihood opportunities—of the blue economies of Africa require a coordinated approach among a wide range of economic sectors. These sectors include fisheries and aquaculture, tourism, renewable energy, marine biotechnology, transport, ports, logistics, wastewater, solid waste management, and environmental protection. Blue Economy activities and projects typically suffer from fragmented policies and budget planning, as well as from limited intersectoral cooperation.

The Blue Economy
According to the African Union, Africa's Blue Economies generated nearly US$300 billion and created close to 50 million jobs in 2018, with economic activities ranging from fisheries to tourism, coastal urban development, trade, and logistics. The African Union's Agenda 2063 has identified the Blue Economy as a key goal towards achieving a prosperous Africa. The potential of Africa's Blue Economy is at risk from a variety of environmental and development pressures, including pollution, fisheries overexploitation, unplanned coastal development, deforestation,

and coastal erosion. Climate change amplifies and accelerates these risks. Communities and ecosystems in coastal Africa are already feeling the impacts of a changing climate. Even with decisive climate action to achieve the Paris goals, these impacts will continue to grow for decades to come. The continent's most vulnerable coastal communities and the fragile marine and coastal ecosystems will need climate adaptation action at scale to prepare for the climate impacts of today and tomorrow.

Higher Education and Capacity Building
In furtherance of its intention to strengthen the scientific competencies and technical capacities in the region, the World Bank is supporting the University of Cape through the Africa Center of Excellence in Coastal Resilience (ACECoR) Project to build capacities of various public and private sector professionals and students for coastal management extension in the areas of climate change, coastal geomorphology and engineering research, Blue economy, Disaster risk management and ecosystems and biodiversity. The focus here is on an improved curriculum, which identifies training goals and learning objectives. So far the project has admitted 120 postgraduate students involving 30 PhDs and 30 Masters' students, drawn from 15 African nations[6]; with a number of other significant Research and Development outputs.[7]

Morphology

Migingo Island, Lake Victoria, Kenya

'The history of human settlements was in coexistence with the natural environment – climate, geology and water bodies.'

Rain season in the Cuvelai Basin, Namibia

Morphology

Africa's lowest lying regions and drainage basins are notably in the north and west of the continent. Informal settlements are mostly spread across eastern to western Africa, with the largest share of urban inhabitants along the Atlantic coast. Coastal African countries have the greatest access to electricity on the continent.

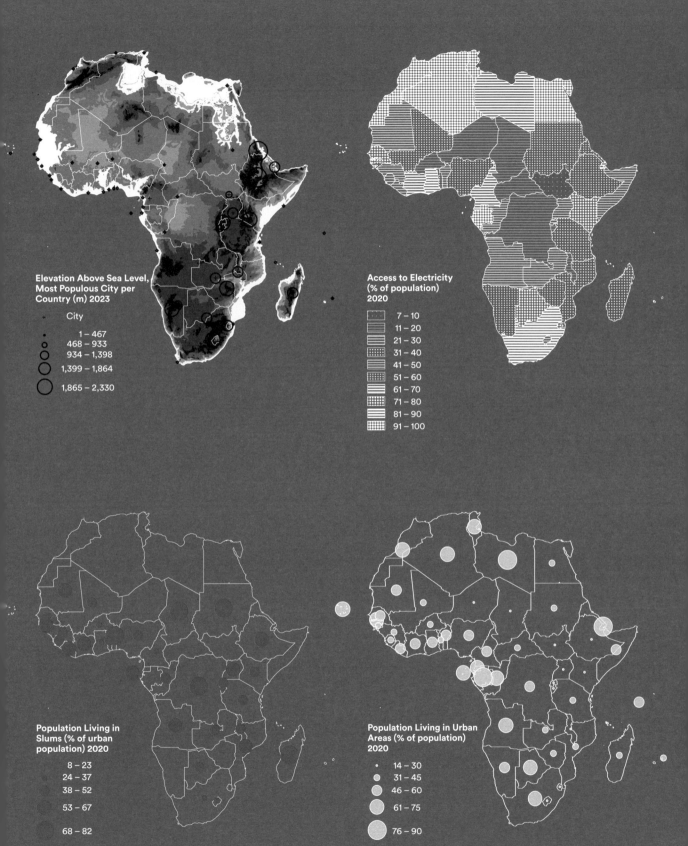

Elevation Above Sea Level, Most Populous City per Country (m) 2023

+ City

· 1 – 467
○ 468 – 933
○ 934 – 1,398
○ 1,399 – 1,864
○ 1,865 – 2,330

Access to Electricity (% of population) 2020

7 – 10
11 – 20
21 – 30
31 – 40
41 – 50
51 – 60
61 – 70
71 – 80
81 – 90
91 – 100

Population Living in Slums (% of urban population) 2020

8 – 23
24 – 37
38 – 52
53 – 67
68 – 82

Population Living in Urban Areas (% of population) 2020

· 14 – 30
31 – 45
46 – 60
61 – 75
76 – 90

COLONIAL TRANSFORMATIONS AND EVOLUTION OF AFRICAN CITIES
Cristina D'Alessandro

Cairo, Egypt

Contemporary African cities and metropolises are generally colonial re-creations of traditional settlements, at least a sizable part of them and especially the large and old ones[1]. There are of course exceptions: Mogadishu, the Somali capital, is over a thousand years old and Aksum is an Ethiopian town that rivalled Rome in antiquity. Pre-colonial empires and other 'political' entities had spatial and social settings that could resemble cities, but they are nowadays considered by scholars as 'city-states', similar by some extent to medieval European cities. Networks and relations between them were in fact generally non-existent or very limited. Most of these pre-colonial cities have been destroyed (for example Benin City, located in the Edo state, in Nigeria, demolished by the British at the end of the nineteenth century) or abandoned by the colonizers (such as Mapungubwe, Zimbabwe, as weather conditions were deemed inappropriate). New cities, recently created for specific functions (i.e. related to oil discoveries, such as Hassi Messaoud, Algeria, or to the mining sector, like Chami, Mauritania, developing through gold mining activities), also exist but they are still exceptions and mostly middle-size cities. Some villages may also grow and become towns, especially border cities developing with commercial exchanges and migration roads. A new port may also transform a remote town in a port city, as could be the case for Port Saint Johns, in South Africa[2].

Contemporary African cities have been generally re-created by the French, the British, the German, the Belgian, and the Portuguese. The colonial system had in fact its own intrinsic interest to build its own urban centres, with specific functions and in precise locations, in line with the overall exploitation trade. Large port cities were then mainly located along the coast, as interfaces, intermediaries, and key connecting places between the inland and the outside world. Globalization was starting already with imperialistic trade, as this system was certainly global, linking various continents through trade. This explains why these cities, developed during the colonial era, have embedded advantages, are still growing and are expected to have a positive demographic trend in the future. They have, in fact, concentrated economic, administrative, and political activities, in addition to infrastructures and services, accumulated over time[3]. The most dynamic, like Dar-es-Salaam, in Tanzania, are also important ports, with commerce drawing a number of other activities. This elucidates why attempts to move inland capital cities of independent states have been challenging and their success often modest. It is still the case for Abuja (far from reaching the size and population of Lagos in Nigeria) and for Yamoussoukro (still less attractive than Abidjan in Cote d'Ivoire).

Other privileged locations were along main rivers, allowing transport of raw materials from the inside to the port: it is the case for Bamako, Mali and Brazzaville, Congo Republic for instance, or Kinshasa, Democratic Republic of Congo. Some cities have been created on a lakeside, such as Kisumu, Kenya or Entebbe, Uganda and benefit from this favourable location for tourism or the fishing industry. A few are located on a plateau, to avoid malaria and other diseases in the past, like Nairobi, in Kenya: its name comes from the Masaai expression Enkare Nairobi ('place of cool waters'). Its site was mistakenly picked, assuming that abundant water was available.

It is then evident, even from this last example, that the location of African cities is, in some way, related to the presence of water, precious in a continent with wide tropical regions, where temperatures can be high, but also rich in water reserves, where the problem is access to rather than availability of water. This tight link of cities with water conditioned urban morphology in the past and still does today, considering the development challenges still confronting African states. Urban morphology is in fact the shape and structure of urban settlements; it includes the logics, but also the process of creation and transformation of urban centres over time: it is what the map or the satellite picture can capture and the reason behind these forms[4]. The presence of a lake, a river, or the ocean is often a physical barrier to the expansion of the city, and generally too difficult to overcome, unless demographic pressures offer conditions to expand thereby, defining its shape.

The first principle inspiring and explaining the shape of colonial cities in Africa was to consider the place, the location chosen, as a tabula rasa. Even if this was not always the case in reality, as indigenous settlements pre-existed in most sites, they were destroyed to obtain an empty and new playground on which to build a city, as imagined and wanted by planners and colonial authorities, according to intrinsic physical and financial limitations. For urban planners, this was a dream situation: to be able to give free rein to their imagination, to invent, and to test possible solutions to local problems, as they could not do in old European cities.

> The presence of a lake, a river, or the ocean is often a physical barrier to the expansion of the city, and generally too difficult to overcome, unless demographic pressures offer conditions to expand thereby, defining its shape.

The second principle was to physically divide the space where the colonizers lived and worked from the locations given to indigenous groups (sometimes attributing each neighbourhood to a unique ethnic group, like in Brazzaville).The 'white city' (the administrative and residential area for the expatriates) was separated from the 'black villages' (as they were often called) by a main avenue that the francophone named *boulevard d'évitement* (avoidance boulevard). This was done for safety reasons (to delay the spread of pandemics) and security reasons (to try to stop the frequent fires). Black neighbourhoods were commonly unplanned and they are the precursors of contemporary slums, but Poto-Poto in Brazzaville shows that there are rare experiments of carefully planned models of indigenous neighbourhoods.

This brings us to the third principle: as only Western European cities were considered at that time real models of urban development and planning, shaped by a long history, African cities have been inspired by ancient urban plans, with a grid-iron street system (following the Roman perpendicular cardo and decumanus division). Western cities inspired monuments, colonial buildings (cf. fascist buildings in Ethiopian cities), and streets, even when the aim was to attempt to create counter-models of urbanism.

From the 1950s and even more rapidly after Independence in the 1960s, rapid urban growth and radical changes of political, economic and social projects for African societies have brought fundamental and numerous changes in urban morphologies around the continent.[5] Beyond this variety, there are some commonalities.

High social and income inequality, tragically common in African societies, dramatically translates nowadays into spatial disparities in urban landscapes, with very diverse demographic densities between highly populated slums and wealthy neighbourhoods with very low density. Inequalities also originate from a different capacity to respond to environmental risks, with slums being disadvantaged by their unfavourable location, but also by poor housing conditions, and widespread poverty.[6] Urban and peri-urban agriculture is in some cases a survival strategy: a response to widespread poverty in urban areas. In other cases, it is a complementary income for middle-class households, willing to improve their living conditions or an option for those not able to rely on public sector salaries.[7] This is a reminder that food security is critical and that local food production and agribusiness are crucial for African cities and countries.

Housing is also a concern and an opportunity in contemporary African cities.[8] Changing and growing needs and new developments are transforming African urban morphology. New housing complexes are built at the outskirts of cities, nearby international airports for instance (for example, the new housing complexes on Bole road in Addis Ababa, Ethiopia, and the Airport Residential Area in Accra, Ghana). Others are built in the 'wholes' inherited from the colonial time . Gated communities flourish for wealthy foreign and local social elites. Growing middle classes in African societies also create new housing needs and openings for constructors and investors, often outside major cities (as is the case in Kenya and in the Democratic Republic of Congo).

Spatial and social inequality makes African cities and their inhabitants more vulnerable to climate change effects. Authorities and experts in charge of urban planning and governance cannot ignore flooding, erosion, and sea level rise,[9] as is the case for the Egyptian Delta's coastal cities. Prevention and protection projects will change urban morphology, as in other parts of the world.[10] They hit dramatically poor and vulnerable neighbourhoods, as in Yaoundé, Cameroon. A multilevel governance mechanism is henceforth needed to have a chance to tackle these issues effectively, like the West Africa Coastal Areas Management Program (WACA) demonstrates. As the Sustainable Development Goals (SDGs) monitoring and evaluation data demonstrate, basic infrastructure and services (including drinking water and sanitation, sewage systems, waste collection[11], but also public transportation, health care and education) are insufficiently developed in African cities and access to them is not universal. A reliable access to affordable electricity is a major challenge not only for private consumption and comfort, but also for development purposes. Financial investment and sustainable economic growth, including in the manufacturing sector, need access to reliable power systems.

Industrial transformation brings new urban morphology models: manufacturing urbanism, including industrial parks[12]. Often located at the outskirts of large metropolises and capital cities (or at a reasonable distance), such as Diamniadio in Dakar, Senegal, or the Bole Lemi Industrial Park, in Addis Ababa, Ethiopia, they concentrate a series of advantages that go far beyond ease of access. Customs duty and other tax exemption, labour force and customer availability, as well as specialized services concentration make them specialized areas of production and trade, particularly attractive for investors and in line with the innovation and competitiveness requirements of the Fourth Industrial Revolution.

As industrialization must be green to be sustainable and competitive, it calls for sustainable urban solutions that African cities are developing and for ownership and innovation to which Africans could contribute more: zero waste strategies, sustainable building materials, smart city projects to reduce congestion and pollution are developing, but boosting the digital sector is critical. Sèmè City is a large campus city under construction in Benin. Based on a triple combination of training, research and entrepreneurship development, the city should enable the emergence of new models of inclusive and sustainable growth through innovation 'Made In Africa'.

This is the process to which African cities could contribute more, if they were properly equipped and if they had the required financing. In fact, the development of capital cities is the necessary and critical step to national development and sustainable economic growth that can radiate from them to the entire country[13].

To conclude, the contemporary fast and deep transformation of urban morphology in African cities includes moving, changing and expanding peri-urban areas, shifting their physical location with the extension of the city, as well as new functions and

composition. Even if it may be increasingly difficult to define what a city is and where it precisely ends, urban spaces are places where urban concentration, diversity and innovation drive dynamics of change.

Spatial and social inequality makes African cities and their inhabitants more vulnerable to climate change effects.

The Nile River flood that hit the capital, Khartoum

'Africa is one of the least responsible but most vulnerable, at the same time, most naturally adaptable to climate change.'

Joal Fadiouth, Senegal

Environment

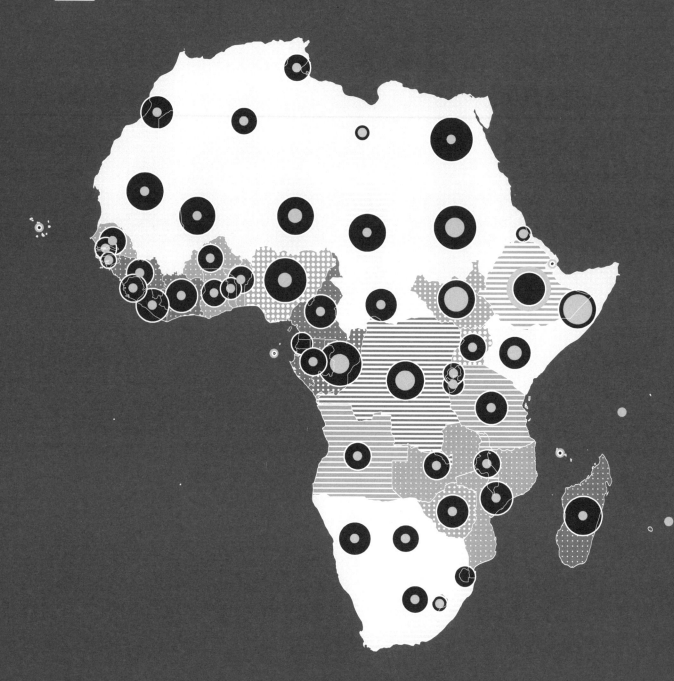

Countries within Africa's equatorial and sub-equatorial tropics experience the largest annual precipitations as well as associated disasters caused by flooding. Urban areas across the continent are exposed to flooding whilst displacement caused by floods, storms and wet mass movements is most common in the horn of Africa.

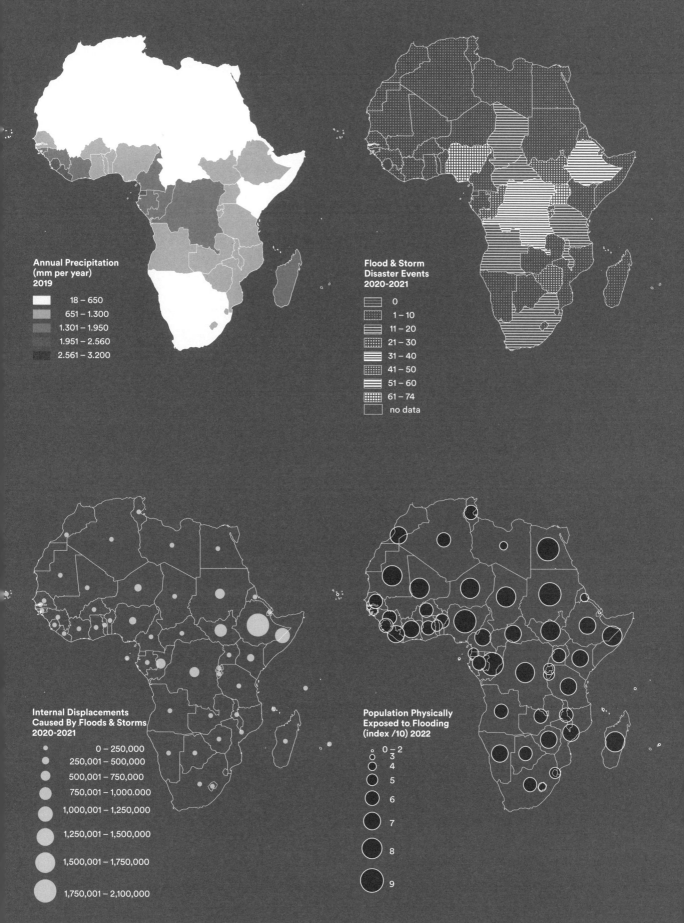

**Annual Precipitation
(mm per year)
2019**

- 18 – 650
- 651 – 1.300
- 1.301 – 1.950
- 1.951 – 2.560
- 2.561 – 3.200

**Flood & Storm
Disaster Events
2020-2021**

- 0
- 1 – 10
- 11 – 20
- 21 – 30
- 31 – 40
- 41 – 50
- 51 – 60
- 61 – 74
- no data

**Internal Displacements
Caused By Floods & Storms
2020-2021**

- 0 – 250,000
- 250,001 – 500,000
- 500,001 – 750,000
- 750,001 – 1,000.000
- 1,000,001 – 1,250,000
- 1,250,001 – 1,500,000
- 1,500,001 – 1,750,000
- 1,750,001 – 2,100,000

**Population Physically
Exposed to Flooding
(index /10) 2022**

- 0 – 2
- 3
- 4
- 5
- 6
- 7
- 8
- 9

THE ENVIRONMENT IN THE WAKE OF CLIMATE CHANGE
Vincent N. Ojeh

An earthwall protects some structures from the flash floods, during the 2022 floods in South Sudan

The trend of urbanization in Africa has been made worse by factors including the natural growth in population, rural-urban movement, conflict, and famine, which force residents to flee within their own countries. People are leaving rural locations for urban centres, most of which are waterfront urban cities. Furthermore, due to the economic opportunities and advantages of African water cities, they tend to be more densely populated than other land uses.

The population of these cities is projected to increase by 3.3 per cent per year between 2000 and 2030, which is twice as fast as the global average. Similarities among African cities influence the degree and mode of their adaptation to climatic whims and catastrophic occurrences. 38 coastal states and several island nations may be found in Africa, including Cape Verde, Sao Tomé and Principe, Mauritius, Seychelles, and Comoros. The vast marine areas that Africa's island nations and shorelines occupy amount to more than 13 million km². While only 31 per cent of West Africa's total population resides in coastal areas, up to 51 per cent of its urban residents do. For instance, Nigeria's coastline area is home to 20 million people, or 22.6 per cent of the nation's overall population. Africa's coasts are where the threat of climate change is greatest right now, claims Mbaye[1].

> Given that coastal communities in Africa are already seeing a noticeable rise in sea level as well as an increase in the frequency and unpredictability of extreme rainfall events, the continent is particularly impacted by climate change.

Currently, flooding affects over 500,000 people annually throughout the region. Sea level rise and coastal erosion are destroying entire villages and towns, costing residents their homes and livelihood. Some areas have seen devastatingly high rates of erosion, between 23 and 30 metres per year, which frequently results in the collapse of national infrastructure such as roads[2]. Lagos, like many other coastal cities, is especially vulnerable to floods and coastal erosion due to the increasing mean sea level rise brought on by climate change.

Environmental Variables Impacting the Growth of African Cities
With Lagos as an example, waterfront cities are by far the most developed metropolitan areas in Africa, and as a result, they are home to a significant number of residential, industrial, commercial, educational and military institutions, and also accommodate transportation and oil and gas infrastructure[3]. Due to their proximity to ports, waterfront development for business and tourism and well-developed coastal and marine environments, these cities have high concentrations of economic activity. Waterfront cities are the primary forces behind the blue economy's expansion. The bulk of these cities is, however, experiencing very rapid economic and population growth, which is known to have negative environmental repercussions because of resource extraction and consumption while natural resources are subjected to increasing amounts of stress.

Cities and Waterfront Neighbourhoods in the Age of Climate Change
Given that coastal communities in Africa are already seeing a noticeable rise in sea level as well as an increase in the frequency and unpredictability of extreme rainfall events, the continent is particularly impacted by climate change. Lagos, Nigeria, is already 30 per cent covered by water bodies[4]. Makoko in Lagos lives on fishing and logging. Makoko, a village of stilted homes, is a prime example of an informal town and waterfront neighbourhood, similar to Ganvie, a developing 'water city' on Lake Nokoué in southern Benin, and Nzulezu in Ghana, which is severely affected by climate change. The Nigerian coast is one of the low-lying regions of Western Africa that is most likely to suffer catastrophic floods as a result of sea level rise and climate change, especially at high tides and during the rainy season[3]. Climate change will undoubtedly pose one of the biggest dangers to Africa's efforts to achieve sustainable development over the next ten years, and nowhere is the threat to the continent's coasts more acute. Numerous dangers, including coastal erosion, storm surges and floods, have an impact on coastal settlements.

Lagos recorded the highest average annual rainfall among the waterfront cities in the past 41 years with a record of 148.6 mm, followed by Abidjan, which recorded 119.8 mm, Dar es Salaam: 92.8 mm; Mombasa: 83.1 mm, Accra: 62.3 mm, Maputo: 59.4 mm; Cape Town: 51.8 mm, Launda:

32.2 mm; Dakar: 21.9 mm and Alexandra: 15.1 mm average annual rainfall respectively. Coupled with the rate of urbanization in these cities, the magnitude of climate-related disasters follows this pattern as well.

These risks are anticipated to worsen as a result of climate change's impact on storm frequency and severity as well as sea level rise[5]. Given the anticipated growth of coastal populations, the seriousness of coastal risks[6] may increase.

> A portion of Lagos has a lot of experience coping with rising water. A large portion of the Makoko neighbourhood is elevated above the water on stilts rather than being built on land.

The most recent assessment from the Intergovernmental Panel on Climate Change (IPCC) lists a number of health implications caused by climate change, including the changed distribution of several infectious illnesses and disease vectors. Due to Lagos' location in a low-lying delta, it is susceptible to seasonal flooding and sea level rise[8]. It has been difficult to adjust the city's vital infrastructure, such as its enormous road network and energy assets, to such changes[9]. In other words, the effects of climate change are being felt in every area of Lagos State, including the following: loss of land to the sea, loss of livelihoods, loss of physical infrastructure (transportation, industrial, energy, water storage and supply, real estate, and so on); displacement of settlements and populations; loss of ecosystems and biodiversity; groundwater and surface water contamination; a rise in the frequency and intensity of climatically associated catastrophes; and a rise in the danger of water-borne illnesses.

Angola recorded 494,200 cases of internal displacement; Côte d'Ivoire: 3,407,000 cases; Egypt: 87,900 cases; Ghana: 277,200 cases; Kenya 1,415,400 cases; Mozambique: 1,363,300 cases; Nigeria: 6,093,300 cases; Senegal: 340,032 cases; Tanzania: 244,800 cases and South Africa: 146,184 cases of internal displacement, conflict and violent disasters respectively between 2008 and 2021. The population in the waterfront cities of these countries bears the highest brunt of environmental and hydrometeorological disasters caused by floods, storms and wet mass movements.

The Adaptation of Waterfront Communities to the Effects of Climate Change

Storms and floods, which currently pose major hazards to the health, lives and livelihoods of the urban poor, will be increasingly common in coastal towns and villages, especially those at low elevations such as Makoko in Lagos, Nzulezu in Ghana, and Ganvie in Benin [10]. Municipal governments will finally need to do what they should have been doing all along: protect the areas where the poor reside so that these areas will have sufficient drainage, secure drinking water supplies and housing resilient enough to resist recurrent flood disasters. How African cities adjust to the projected effects of climate change will have a significant impact on how humankind will fare[10]. Although Lagos and Lagosians may already be adapting to climate change in a variety of ways, due to the complexity and urgency of the issue as well as the power of inertia, which prevents people from quickly changing from their routines, the government launched the Lagos State Climate Change Adaptation Strategy (LAS-CCAS) to provide a ready tool for implementing a regime of guided, coordinated change for the rapid responses required to reduce climate change in Lagos covering the 2020–2025 climate adaptation plan.

A portion of Lagos has a lot of experience coping with rising water. A large portion of the Makoko neighbourhood is elevated above the water on stilts rather than being built on land. Makoko, dubbed the 'Venice of Africa', is a maze-like slum that can only be reached by boat. The slum has limited access to power and sanitary facilities, but it has also produced inventions like the Makoko Floating School (Plate 1), a building that is buoyantly supported by repurposed empty plastic barrels. The pyramidal design of the school reduced its centre of gravity, improved stability, and provided a perfect form for the roof to shed heavy rains (Johnson, 2021).

Current and Future Environmental Challenges and Opportunities for African Water Cities

Lagos' high susceptibility to climate change has been shown by substantial damage from floods and storms, as in most other waterfront cities on the African continent. Such vulnerabilities are made worse by the city's position, together with vital infrastructure that is insufficient and badly maintained, and weak urban governance. While it is evident that Lagos' high vulnerability to the effects of climate change has prompted government responses and policy attention, implementation and coordination across various scales still need significant upgrading, with a focus on fairness and involvement in decision-making[9].

The difficulty of managing municipal urban garbage in Lagos is another issue that affects the state's capacity for adaptation to climate change as well as the ability of Lagosians to do so. Lagos State is a naturally growing city that has expanded without a sufficient strategy to accommodate the growing population. It has impacted the services provided as well as the infrastructure system's quality and longevity. The population boom and haphazard urbanization outpace the shoddy infrastructure and waste management services. As a result, piles of solid trash are allowed to be burned, flushed into drainage systems and canals, and carelessly deposited in public areas and open landfills[11]. Recent studies indicate that many countries have forgotten to plan for the solid waste sector when creating their policies for adapting to the changing climate and do not include it in their Nationally Determined Contributions (NDCs)[12]. Numerous studies have found that efforts to adapt to climate change in cities throughout the world are hampered by governance problems brought on by divergent viewpoints, roles, and duties[13]. Today, Lagos is plagued by several issues, including disease outbreaks, coastal erosion and flooding, forced evictions, economic downturn, building collapse, high unemployment and underemployment, traffic congestion, inadequate physical and social infrastructure, an inadequate transportation system, formal-informal economic competition, erratic power supply, civil unrest, urban fires, and a weak public health system[14].

Despite the challenges associated with Africa's water cities, there is a huge opportunity for them in the blue economy as the world moves towards net zero carbon emission production. According to the World Bank, the blue economy has the potential to generate employment for Africa's expanding population while assisting with climate adaptation and mitigation efforts.

Despite the challenges associated with Africa's water cities, there is a huge opportunity for them in the blue economy as the world moves towards net zero carbon emission production.

Resources

Thousands of contestants for the annual Argungu fishing festival search for the largest fish in the River Rima

'Some of Africa's largest freshwater sources continue to shrink, increasing the paradox of scarcity and abundance.'

Barge with logs on the Congo River

Resources

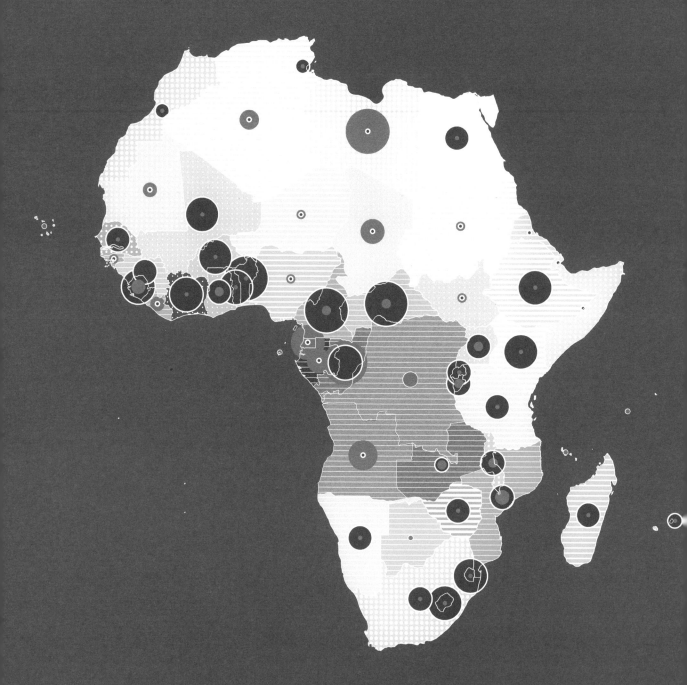

Africa's equatorial and sub-equatorial zones have the largest share of forest land on the continent. Here, the export of agricultural merchandise is high. Income from natural resources as a percentage of GDP is high in central Africa whilst arid and semi-arid zones in northern, eastern and southern Africa experience the most water stress.

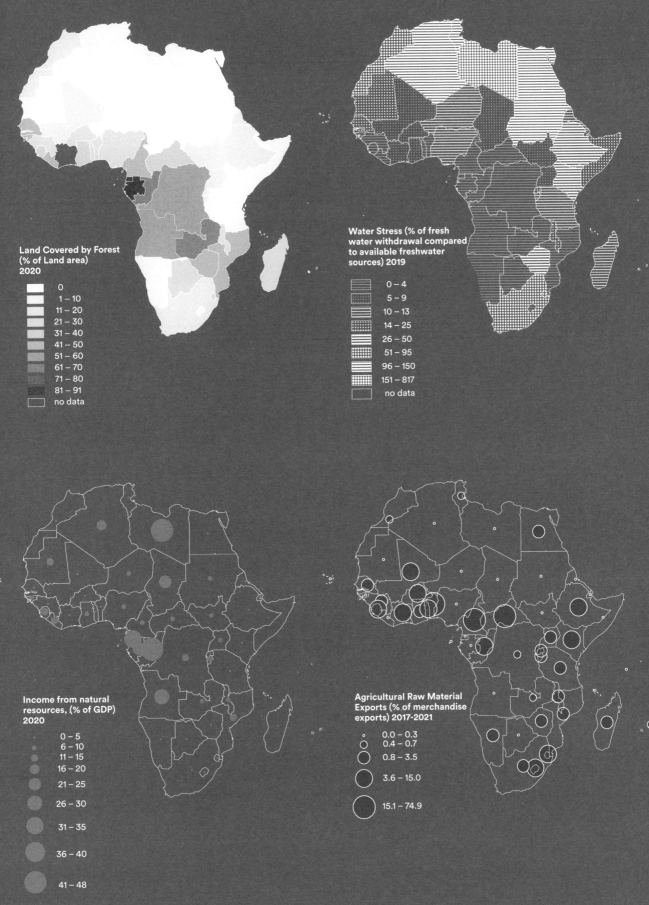

**Land Covered by Forest
(% of Land area)
2020**

- 0
- 1 – 10
- 11 – 20
- 21 – 30
- 31 – 40
- 41 – 50
- 51 – 60
- 61 – 70
- 71 – 80
- 81 – 91
- no data

**Water Stress (% of fresh
water withdrawal compared
to available freshwater
sources) 2019**

- 0 – 4
- 5 – 9
- 10 – 13
- 14 – 25
- 26 – 50
- 51 – 95
- 96 – 150
- 151 – 817
- no data

**Income from natural
resources, (% of GDP)
2020**

- 0 – 5
- 6 – 10
- 11 – 15
- 16 – 20
- 21 – 25
- 26 – 30
- 31 – 35
- 36 – 40
- 41 – 48

**Agricultural Raw Material
Exports (% of merchandise
exports) 2017-2021**

- 0.0 – 0.3
- 0.4 – 0.7
- 0.8 – 3.5
- 3.6 – 15.0
- 15.1 – 74.9

THE IMPACT OF URBANIZATION ON THE LAKE CHAD BASIN

Ngozi Finette Unuigbe and
Violet Omon Aigbokhaevbo

N'Djamena, Chad

Despite contributing a minute amount to global greenhouse gas emissions[1], Africa has been at the receiving end of ongoing and impending effects of climate change. Agriculture, the mainstay of African rural economies, has also been greatly affected as deforestation and prolonged absence of rainfall have become prevalent in many regions. Temperatures in Africa are also projected to peak higher than the global temperature increase, which spells doom for the continent as every bit of global warming adds greater risks in the form of droughts, heat waves, food scarcity, poverty, and crop failures[2]. This situation may further worsen as the continent gradually urbanizes without proper city structures. Already, urban centres consume most of the world's energy supply and are responsible for around 70 per cent of global energy-related greenhouse gas emissions. This invariably means that in the next five to ten years, the lives and livelihood of millions of people will be affected by what is done (or not done) in urban centres with regard to the climate[3]. Forecasts from the World Economic Forum suggests that by 2050, Africa's population may have doubled and more than 80 per cent of that increase will occur in cities, especially in slums[4].

A textbook example of how climate change could lead to increased urbanization is the deplorable condition of the Lake Chad Basin [5]. Between the mid-1960s and 1980s, the LCB lost about 90 per cent of its surface area water (over 23,000 square kilometres) and has currently been reduced to less than 1,500 square kilometres[6]. Prior to the climate crisis, the lake could boast on being one of the largest freshwater bodies in Africa, supporting the livelihood of millions of people from various countries sharing its transboundary resource[7]. The vast majority of the population there (80-90 per cent[8]) engage in either agriculture, cattle farming or fishing, all of which largely thrive on the availability of the natural resources that the LCB provides—water and fertile land. The lake also supports wildlife conservation and acts as a vital source for food security around the region. There are many reasons for the drying up of the Lake, including unsustainable irrigation projects, a drop in annual rainfall, overgrazing, deforestation, and population growth, which in turn leads to an exorbitant exploitation of water resources. With the desiccation of water sources in the LCB, millions of persons have lost their livelihood. As a consequence, habitants have been forced to migrate to more stable environments where security and better opportunities were assured. As rural settlements are both lacking in opportunities and resilience to adapt to climate change, there has been an increased influx of persons migrating to growing urban areas around the LCB. The growing effects of this urbanization has its effect on climate change and if not controlled, could exacerbate the already devastating conditions of the region.

How Urbanization Will Affect the Lake Chad Basin
The climatic conditions of the LCB will have significant effects on the local economy around it as well as around its tributaries (Chadi and Logone). These effects largely explain how urbanization will shape the future of the Lake in two major ways. Firstly, as climate change persists, people will be forced to migrate to urban areas, which would eventually lead to overcrowding and could in turn have adverse effects on climate change in the region. Secondly, the climate change may empower smaller towns to gradually urbanize, as the search for waters around the Lake may lead to incessant migration of the Lake's wildlife and riparian populations[9]. Both have their downsides, which is further exacerbating the already deplorable condition of the LCB. Urbanization in the LCB is already happening as populations in some of its towns are outpacing the global average urbanization rate[10]. One of the riparian states, Nigeria, is predicted by the United Nations to account for more than a third of the global urban population by 2050, alongside China and India[11]. Also, smaller towns around the LCB have witnessed a doubling of their populations in less than a decade. For instance, the Nigerian town of Gwoza grew by 42 per cent to a population of 69,000 between 2010-2015. Towns such as Damaturu, Mubi and Gambaru have witnessed explosive population growth in the past two decades[12]. This suggests the need for adequate attention to support growing cities.

Urban development is critical to the environment in many ways, as it affects natural vegetation by replacing it with surfaces that are impermeable and inflexible to the movement of water and air. These replacements of green areas have effects on rainfall, temperature and the relative humidity in an area. Overpopulation of the urban area may also lower nocturnal radiation, releasing more carbon, which is likely to increase the effects of climate change. In addition, urbanization may also lead to general temperature increase, causing 'urban warming', and other complications such as flooding, drought, and air pollution. The majority of the people migrating in the LCB struggle to sustain a livelihood, and their numbers may largely account for increased slum population in urban centres. Overcrowded slums have adverse effects on climate as areas like these are usually affected by water scarcity and air pollution. Lower quality and poorly designed buildings in slums are also strong factors for landslides and floods during rainfall[13]. Already, urban centres in the LCB such as Maiduguri in northeast Nigeria and Maroua in Cameroon host vast numbers of rural migrants in the region[14]. If improperly managed, the climate crisis in these areas and other growing urban areas may worsen and have far-reaching effects on smaller towns across the Lake.

The Way Forward

As smaller towns around the LCB are gradually urbanizing, much attention should be given to proper city structuring with emphasis on mitigating the risks of climate change. A viable approach is the practice of conservative agriculture with emphasis on promoting improved irrigation methods and practices to ensure water saving and the recycling of lower quality/drainage water for use. Urban centres in the LCB should also focus on building sustainable green cities, built on the back of afforestation and maintenance of natural vegetation through the construction of parks and gardens. Already, some communities, such as Liwa, Merea and Tantevrom, have been engaging in the planting of drought-tolerant seedlings (acacia trees) over a large expanse of land.[15] Research should also be done on the potential of cities in the LCB to generate and rely on renewable energy sources for industrialization processes as opposed to the use of fossil fuels.

On a policy level, countries sharing the transboundary water resource of the Lake Chad basin (Nigeria, Chad, Niger and Cameroon) should not renege on fulfilling their Nationally Determined Contributions (NDCS) to the United Nations Framework Convention on Climate Change (UNFCCC) with more ambitious adaptation and mitigation targets.[16] The COP27[17] has clearly set out the need for climate finance, and the sustainability of the LCB will largely depend on the collective, committed efforts of the region's government to ensure sustainable climate practices. Also, there is a need for increased advocacy by the Lake Chad Basin commission[18] and the governments of the region to push for climate awareness among the population of the LCB and the international community. This is imperative, as global urbanization may account for the drying up of waters in the LCB.

Some actions have been taken to ensure sustainable climate practices in the LCB. For instance, in 2017, a financing agreement was reached between UNESCO and the Lake Chad Basin states to sustainably manage the hydrological, biological and cultural resources of the Lake across their borders in order to support poverty reduction and promote peace.[19] Previously, in 2008, UNDP had supported the LCBC in carrying out a diagnostic analysis, which led to the development of a Strategic Action Programme (SAP). Currently, the LCBC is on a mission to implement the SAP to achieve a climate-resilient and integrated ecosystem through implementation of agreed policy, legal and institutional reforms, and investments that improve water quality and quantity, protect biodiversity, and sustain livelihoods.[20] Also, there is an existing water charter[21] which seeks to bind the LCBC states to cooperate in achieving the sustainable management of water resources in Lake Chad by complying with rules and principles governing international lakes and water courses. Nigeria, Chad and Cameroon are also signatories to the UN water convention[22], which suggests intentions by member states to develop recognized sustainable water practices.

To conclude, although it is a given that the process of urbanization is largely influenced by local climatic conditions, urban development has introduced changes in land surface characteristics which has gradually turned the local climate into an 'urban climate'[23]. It goes without saying that if urban centres are improperly structured, the climate conditions in the LCB may worsen. On the other hand, urban centres possess the resilience, financial grit and coping mechanisms to deal with the deplorable climate conditions in the LCB.

Fishermen in two canoes on the waters of Lake Chad

TOP 20 AFRICAN WATER CITIES

PORTO DE S.VIC

CABO

$ $50

CORREIOS

VERDE

Porto de S. Vicente Cabo Verde | Postage Stamp | Year: 1972

METHODOLOGY

The Top 20 African Water Cities is an empirical ranking and index of major African cities and capitals that highlights the cities that are at the epicentres of issues of urbanization and climate change in Africa. These are the twenty cities that would have the most significant challenges as well as the greatest opportunities for urbanization and climate change based on the 'Seven DESIMER Factors of Sustainable Urban development' — a unique research methodology developed by African Water Cities to evaluate the dynamics that drive developments particularly the complex socio-economic and environmental realities of African cities and communities. DESIMER is an acronym for Demographics, Economics, Socio-Politics, Infrastructure, Morphology, Environment and Resources and the Top 20 African Water Cities is based on data that is constantly evolving but this provides a snapshot and synthesis of various data mostly over the last 20 years.

These datasets (four for each of the seven DESIMER factors, 28 in total) also correlate with values and indicators of sustainable development – 'development that meets the needs of the present without compromising the ability of future generations to meet their own needs', as defined by the UN and the 17 Sustainable Development Goals (SDG).

To index cities within the seven factors of urban development, raw figures are converted to a value up to 100 relative only to the data in the index. 100 is the maximum 'potential impact' score for cities and countries experiencing the greatest demographic transitions, economic strength, financial support, environmental vulnerability and socio-political capability to implement change. The maximum score is 2800. The Top 20 African Water Cities are therefore the highest-ranking cities based on a result of this empirical DESIMER data collection and mapping.

In the dawn of AI and as early adopters of innovation, each of the top 20 African Water Cities is presented through a short story by the technological tool currently arousing global interests: ChatGPT. Its outputs are generated by machine learning through language models and may include inaccuracies. These short-stories are coupled with facts drawn from the compiled datasets and bring to the fore questions of access, information gaps, and the increasingly ambiguous territory between reality and fiction.

Demographics

Economics

Socio-politics

Infrastructure

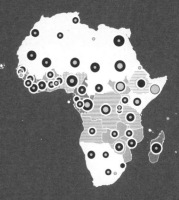

Environment

Morphology

Resources

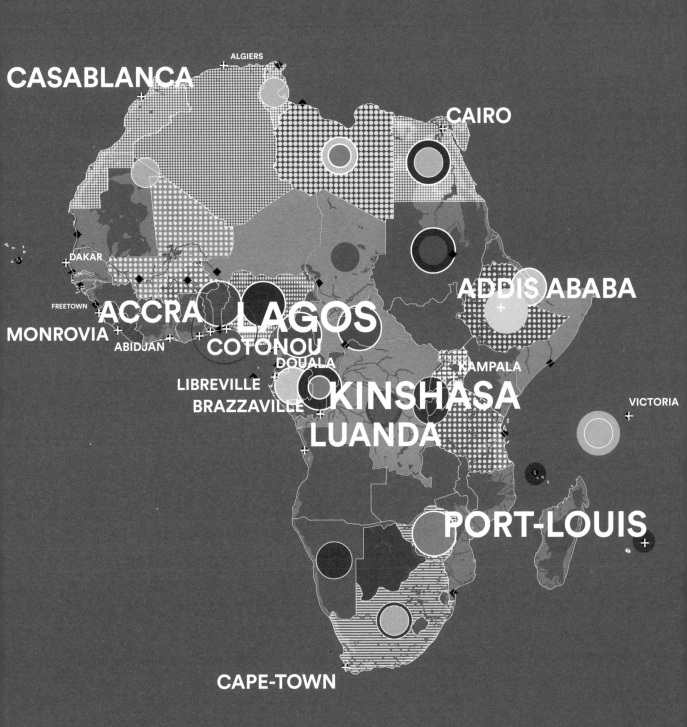

CASABLANCA

ALGIERS

CAIRO

DAKAR

FREETOWN

MONROVIA

ACCRA

ABIDJAN

COTONOU

LAGOS

LIBREVILLE

DOUALA

BRAZZAVILLE

KINSHASA

LUANDA

ADDIS ABABA

KAMPALA

VICTORIA

PORT-LOUIS

CAPE-TOWN

DESIMER is an acronym for Demographics, Economics, Socio-Politics, Infrastructure, Morphology, Environment and Resources. The Top 20 African Water Cities is based on data that are constantly evolving; it is a synthesis of various data mostly from the last 20 years.

TOP 20 AFRICAN WATER CITIES

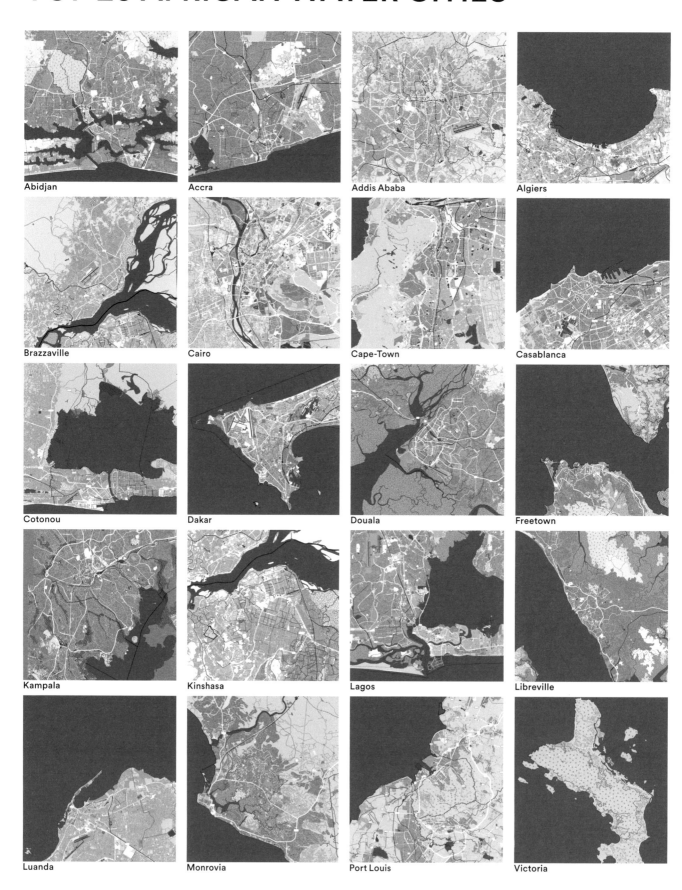

Abidjan

Accra

Addis Ababa

Algiers

Brazzaville

Cairo

Cape-Town

Casablanca

Cotonou

Dakar

Douala

Freetown

Kampala

Kinshasa

Lagos

Libreville

Luanda

Monrovia

Port Louis

Victoria

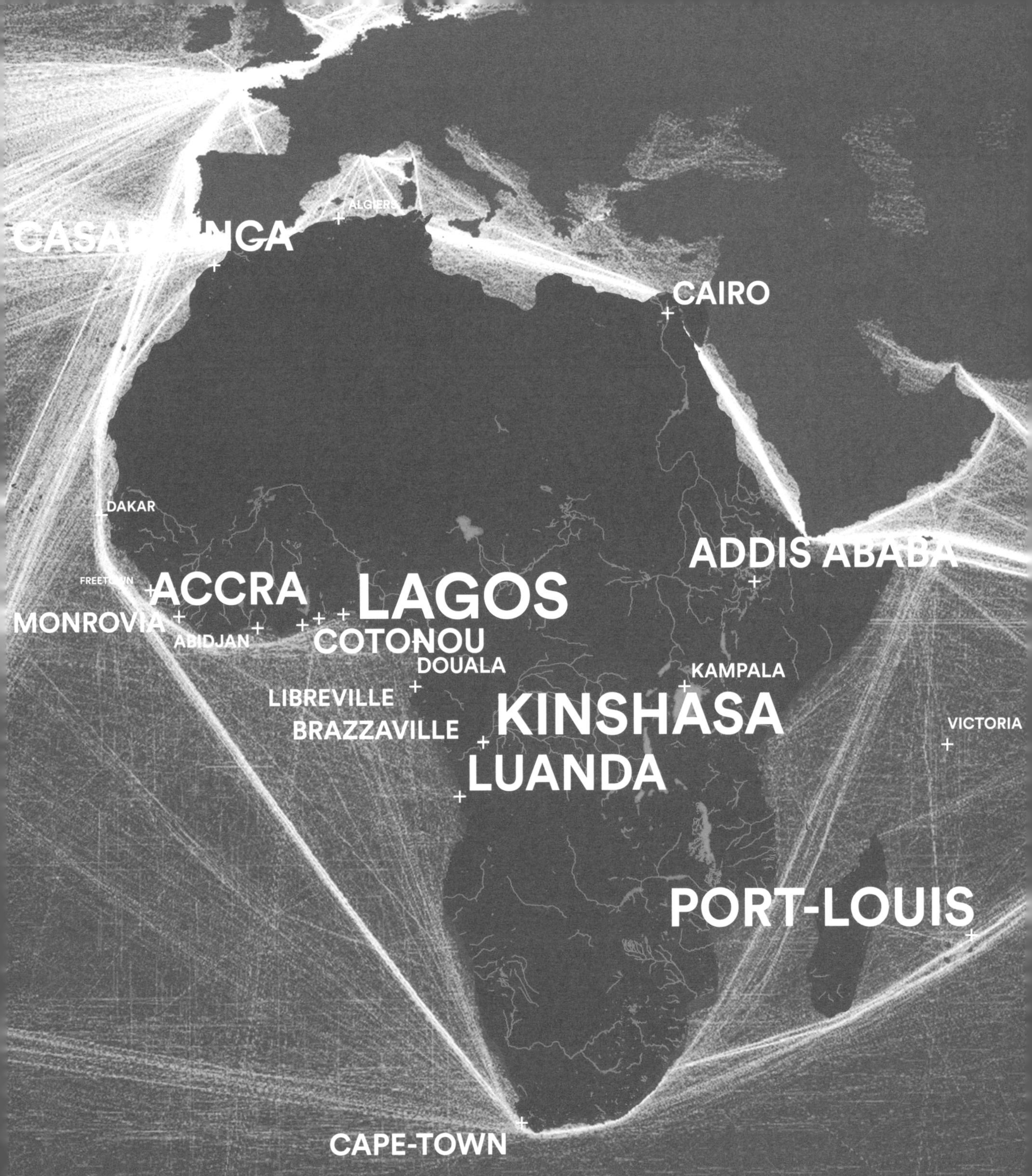

CASABLANCA
ALGIERS
CAIRO
DAKAR
ADDIS ABABA
FREETOWN
ACCRA
LAGOS
MONROVIA
ABIDJAN
COTONOU
DOUALA
KAMPALA
LIBREVILLE
VICTORIA
BRAZZAVILLE
KINSHASA
LUANDA
PORT-LOUIS
CAPE-TOWN

The Top 20 African Water Cities are the cities that face the most significant
challenges as a result of climate change, but also with the greatest
opportunities for urbanization.

Urban floods in Lagos, Nigeria

FLOODING IN AFRICAN WATER CITIES

Abidjan

Accra

Addis Ababa

Algiers

Brazzaville

Cairo

Cape-Town

Casablanca

Cotonou

Dakar

Douala

Freetown

Kampala

Kinshasa

Lagos

Libreville

Luanda

Monrovia

Port Louis

Victoria

AFRICAN WATER CITIES

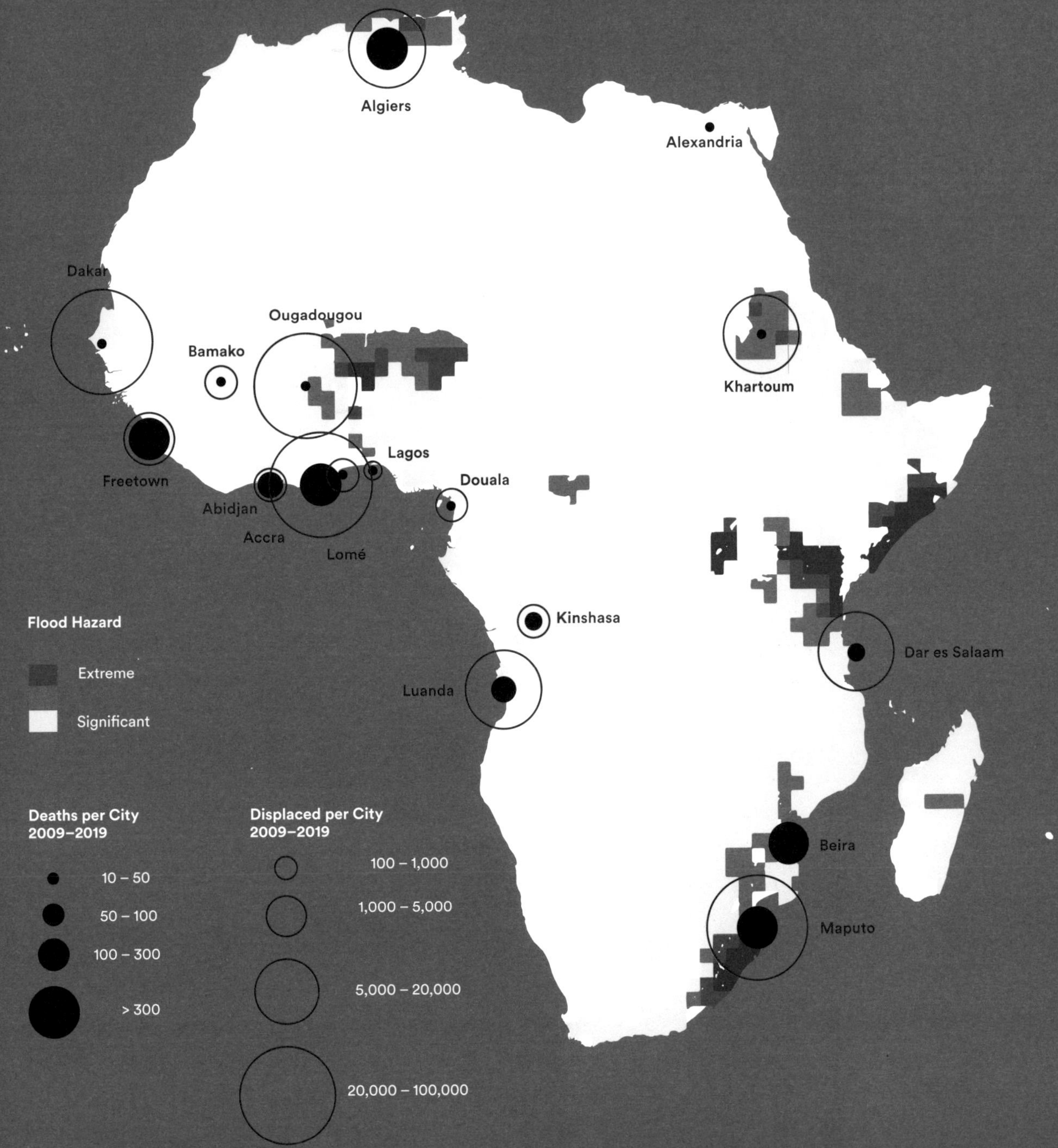
Algiers
Alexandria
Dakar
Ougadougou
Bamako
Khartoum
Lagos
Freetown
Douala
Abidjan
Accra
Lomé
Kinshasa
Dar es Salaam
Luanda
Beira
Maputo
Flood Hazard
Extreme
Significant
Deaths per City 2009–2019
10 – 50
50 – 100
100 – 300
> 300
Displaced per City 2009–2019
100 – 1,000
1,000 – 5,000
5,000 – 20,000
20,000 – 100,000

Urban flood types can be categorized as: 'fluvial' or river flooding - occurring when water flow exceeds capacity of rivers, canals or other channels; 'pluvial' or overland, caused by insufficient penetrable ground surfaces or lack of drainage systems, coastal floods due to storms, and groundwater floods that happen when water table rises due to increased rainfall.

Abidjan is the economic capital of Côte d'Ivoire, a country located in West Africa. The Ébrié Lagoon is a large lagoon that is situated along the southern coast of Côte d'Ivoire, just east of Abidjan. It is fed by the Comoé River, and it is home to a diverse array of aquatic life, including fish, crabs and shrimp. The Vridi Canal is an artificial waterway that connects the Ébrié Lagoon to the Gulf of Guinea, allowing for ships to enter and exit the port of Abidjan. The Vridi Canal is a critical infrastructure for the economic development of Côte d'Ivoire and the West African region. It plays a significant role in the country's import and export activities, as well as the transport of goods and materials for industries such as oil and gas, mining, and agriculture.

ABIDJAN, Côte d'Ivoire

Between 2005-2020, Côte d'Ivoire was one of the fastest-growing economies in Africa. The country has a high-performing logistics infrastructure, making it attractive for investment and expansion.

7.8m   2.89/5 $1.03   5.95%

Accra, the capital city of Ghana, is situated on the Atlantic coast, making the ocean a crucial aspect of the city's identity and economy. The ocean provides a vital source of fish and seafood for the city's residents, and the fishing industry is a significant employer. Additionally, the port of Tema, located near Accra, is one of the largest ports in West Africa, handling goods from around the world. The ocean also attracts tourists who visit the city to enjoy its beaches and water-based activities such as surfing and swimming. The Atlantic Ocean is thus an essential part of Accra's economic and cultural landscape, highlighting the need for its sustainable management and conservation.

ACCRA
Ghana

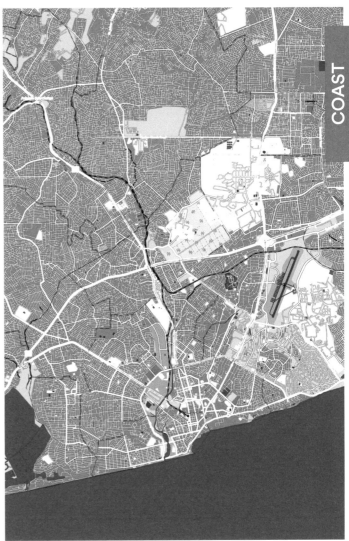

COAST

Over half of Ghana's population live in urban areas and the majority of the country's population has access to electricity. In 2020, the country's negative net FDI (Foreign Direct Investment) was notably much larger than the continental average.

2m
city population
2022

57%
pop. live in urban areas

$0.64
bottled water

-1.3B
FDI (net) 2020

Addis Ababa is the capital city of Ethiopia, located in the central highlands of the country. The city is not situated on any major rivers or water bodies but sits within a plateau surrounded by several water bodies, including the Awash River and several small lakes and springs. These impact and shape the city's environment and economy. The Gefersa Reservoir is located just outside of Addis Ababa and is the primary source of water for the city. The Ayat Reservoir is located within the city limits and provides water to the eastern part of the city. The management and conservation of these water bodies are essential to ensure a sustainable supply of drinking water and to protect the city's biodiversity and economic activities.

ADDIS ABABA
Ethiopia

Between 2005 and 2020, Ethiopia experienced the fastest economic growth in Africa coupled with high urban population growth. The country's population is exposed to floods and storms which caused the highest rates of internal displacement on the continent from 2020-2021.

15.4m
city population
2022

2.1m
IDPs from floods &
storms 2020-2021

$0.65
bottled water

9.9%
economic growth
2005-2020

Algiers is the capital and largest city of Algeria, which is located in North Africa. Algiers is situated on the Bay of Algiers, which is an inlet of the Mediterranean Sea. The city has a long history of maritime trade. It is also known for its historical significance as it has been inhabited by various civilizations throughout its history. Although not major sources of water for the city, several small rivers play an important role in the city's environmental ecology and recreation along their banks. The primary source of water for Algiers is obtained from nearby reservoirs. These serve a variety of purposes, including irrigation, flood control, hydroelectric power generation, and water supply. As one of the largest ports in North Africa, the Port of Algiers serves as a major gateway and its strategic location makes it a vital transportation hub for goods moving between Europe, Africa, and the Middle East.

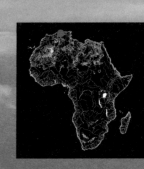

ALGIERS
Algeria

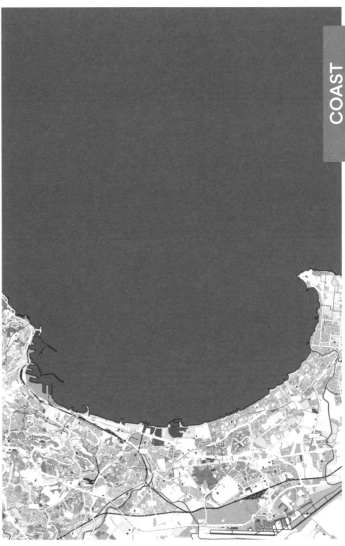

Most of Algeria's population live in urban areas and nearly the whole population has access to electricity. Between 2005 - 2020, the country experienced relatively slow economic growth, below the continental average.

2m
city population
2022

1.06
tonnes per capita

$0.38
bottled water

99.8%
electricity access
2020

Brazzaville is the capital and largest city of the Republic of the Congo, which is located in Central Africa. It is situated on the north bank of the Congo River, directly across from the city of Kinshasa in the neighbouring Democratic Republic of the Congo. The river is a vital transportation route for goods and people, with boats and barges transporting goods such as timber, minerals and agricultural products to markets downstream. It is also an important source of hydroelectric power, with several large dams along the river providing electricity to the region. The Congo River also plays an important cultural and social role in the lives of Brazzaville's residents, with many activities and celebrations taking place on or near the river. The river is also home to a diverse range of aquatic and terrestrial species, including many endemic species found nowhere else in the world.

BRAZZAVILLE
Republic of the Congo

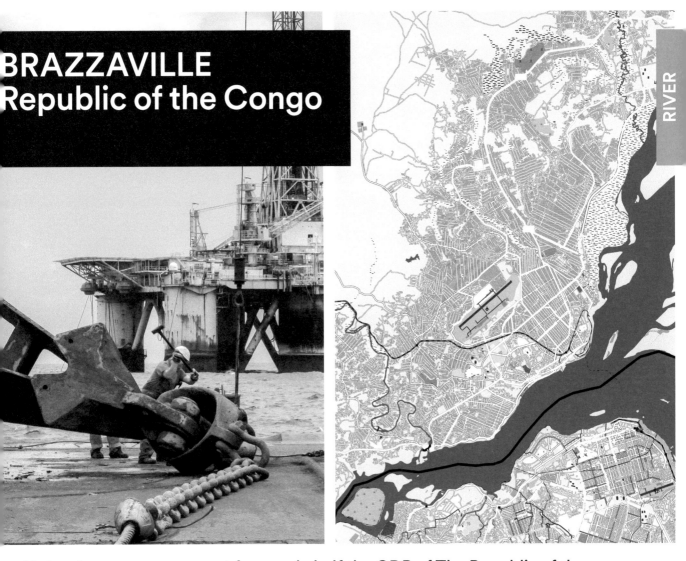

RIVER

Natural resources account for nearly half the GDP of The Republic of the Congo. This is the largest percentage in Africa. In 2022, the country's population was most exposed to flooding on the continent.

1.3m
city population
2022

57%
pop. live in urban areas
2020

$1.07
bottled water

48%
income from natural
resources 2020

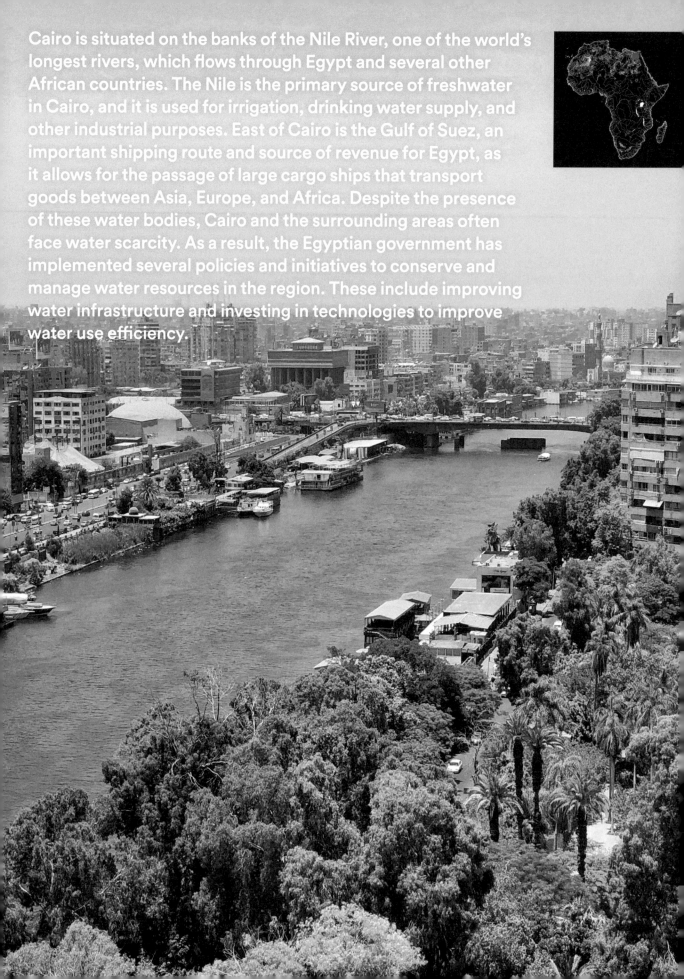

Cairo is situated on the banks of the Nile River, one of the world's longest rivers, which flows through Egypt and several other African countries. The Nile is the primary source of freshwater in Cairo, and it is used for irrigation, drinking water supply, and other industrial purposes. East of Cairo is the Gulf of Suez, an important shipping route and source of revenue for Egypt, as it allows for the passage of large cargo ships that transport goods between Asia, Europe, and Africa. Despite the presence of these water bodies, Cairo and the surrounding areas often face water scarcity. As a result, the Egyptian government has implemented several policies and initiatives to conserve and manage water resources in the region. These include improving water infrastructure and investing in technologies to improve water use efficiency.

**CAIRO
Egypt**

RIVER

By 2020, Egypt had the largest percentage of formal settlement and electricity access in Africa. In 2019, the country had the lowest levels of rainfall on the continent, yet Egypt's population is one of the most at risk of flooding on the continent.

7.7m
city population
2022

0.2m
rainfall per year
2019

$0.41
bottled water

141%
water stress 2019

Cape Town is a coastal city located in the Western Cape Province of South Africa. It is the legislative capital of South Africa and the second-most populous city in the country. Shipping makes an important contribution to the city's economy and the coastal climate supports tourism year-round. Cape Town, like many other cities in South Africa, experiences periodic water shortages due to its location in a semi-arid region and its growing population. Cape Town does not have major rivers flowing through but is prone to flooding during the winter months, particularly in low-lying areas. The city relies on water sources such as the Theewaterskloof Dam: This is the largest dam in the Western Cape and is located on the Sonderend River, supplying water to Cape Town and other surrounding towns.

CAPE TOWN
South Africa

South Africa has one of the highest performing trade and logistics sectors in Africa and the country's gender gap is one of the smallest. In 2020 South Africa had the second largest negative FDI on the continent.

3.4m
city population
2022

2.89/5
logistics performance 2018

$1.20
bottled water

78/100
gender equality
2021

Casablanca is a coastal city located in western Morocco. It has a Mediterranean climate with mild, wet winters and hot, dry summers. The city is situated on the Atlantic Coastal Plain, which is a flat and relatively low-lying area that extends along the Atlantic coast of Morocco, bordered by the Atlas Mountains to the east and the Atlantic Ocean to the west. The main surface water resources in Casablanca include the Oum Er-Rbia River. This is the largest river in Morocco, and it originates from the Middle Atlas Mountains, flowing westwards into the Atlantic Ocean. The river provides an important source of freshwater for agriculture, industry, and domestic use in Casablanca and the surrounding region. Casablanca also has one of the largest and busiest ports in North Africa.

CASABLANCA
Morocco

Most of Morocco's urban inhabitants live in formal housing. In 2020, the country also boasted the most electricity, internet access and container port traffic on the continent.

3.1m
city population
2022

84%
internet usage 2020

$0.73
bottled water

7m
equiv. 20ft containers
moved in 2020

Cotonou is the largest city and economic capital of Benin, located on the coast of the Gulf of Guinea, an arm of the Atlantic Ocean. There are several lakes and lagoons in the surrounding region. Lake Nokoué is a large freshwater lake located to the north of Cotonou. It is connected to the Atlantic Ocean by a channel and is an important fishing ground for local communities and several traditional fishing villages. The Ouémé River is a major river that runs through southern Benin and flows into the Atlantic Ocean just east of Cotonou. The river is important for irrigation and hydroelectric power generation whilst Cotonou Port serves as a major gateway for trade in the region, connecting Benin and its neighbouring landlocked countries to the global market.

MARCHE DANTOKPA

COTONOU
Benin

In 2021, Benin's agricultural export as a share of merchandise exports was larger than that of any other country across the continent. Cotonou is a notably low-lying city and the country's population live predominantly in informal settlements.

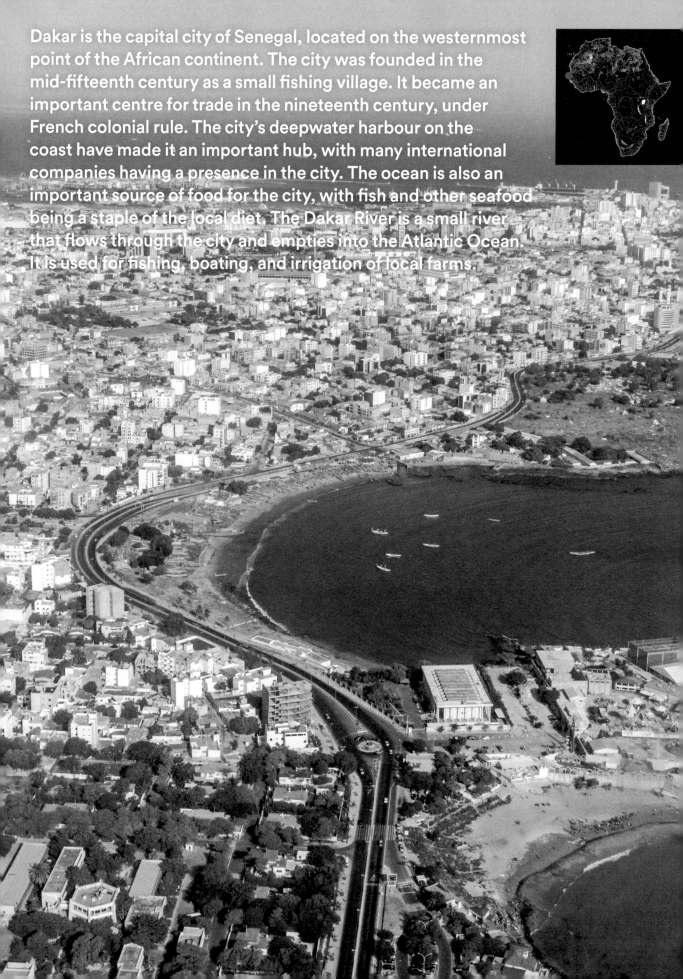

Dakar is the capital city of Senegal, located on the westernmost point of the African continent. The city was founded in the mid-fifteenth century as a small fishing village. It became an important centre for trade in the nineteenth century, under French colonial rule. The city's deepwater harbour on the coast have made it an important hub, with many international companies having a presence in the city. The ocean is also an important source of food for the city, with fish and other seafood being a staple of the local diet. The Dakar River is a small river that flows through the city and empties into the Atlantic Ocean. It is used for fishing, boating, and irrigation of local farms.

DAKAR
Senegal

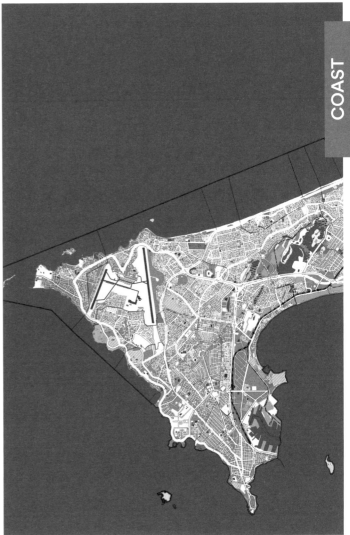

Dakar has a larger population than most capital cities in Africa. Senegal's container port traffic is higher than the continental median, but a relatively low share of export comes from raw agriculture materials.

2.5m
city population
2022

1.2%
exports from raw agriculture
materials 2021

$0.86
bottled water

563k
equiv. 20ft containers
moved in 2020

Douala is the largest city in Cameroon and the capital of its Littoral Region. The city is located on the Wouri River in the southwestern part of the country. It is a major economic centre serving as the commercial capital of Cameroon and the Central African region. The river is an important source of water for Douala and the surrounding region, and it is used for a variety of purposes, including irrigation, fishing, and transportation. The river and its associated wetlands are home to a diverse array of plant and animal life. The Wouri River is also an important economic and cultural resource for the region, and it is likely to be an important factor in the city's development and growth.

DOUALA
Cameroon

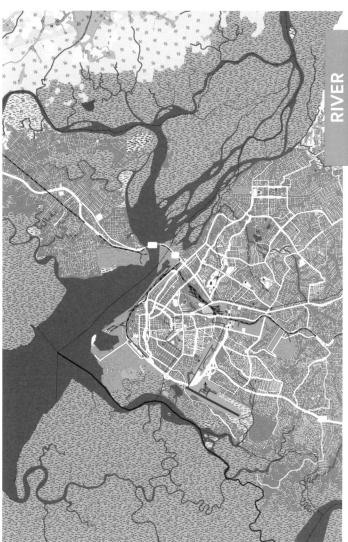

Cameroon's GDP per capita is just above the continental median. The country has a good logistics sector. Excluding aviation and shipping, the country's CO_2 emissions from transport in relation to GDP were below the continental median in 2019.

1.3m
city population
2022

0.13
tonnes per capita
from transport 2019

$0.92
bottled water

$3.7k
GDP per capita ppp 2021

Freetown is the capital city of Sierra Leone, located on the western coast of Africa. The Atlantic Ocean and the bay play a role in its climate, with warm, humid weather year-round. They are an important source of food for the city, with fish and other seafood being a staple of the local diet. The city's location on the coast has made it an important hub for commerce, tourism and recreational activities. The Sierra Leone River is the largest river in Sierra Leone and flows into the Atlantic Ocean near Freetown. The Guma Dam, a large reservoir located in the hills outside of the city, is the primary source of water for the city, providing up to 70 percent of the city's water supply.

FREETOWN
Sierra Leone

Sierra Leone had one of the strictest Covid-19 protocols. The country has some of the most precipitation on the continent and is notably exposed to flooding, yet no disasters were recorded in 2020-2021.

0.8m
city population
2022

45/100
covid containment strictness
dec. 2022

$0.91
bottled water

2.5m
annual percipitation 2019

Kampala is the capital and largest city of Uganda, a country located in East Africa. It is situated on the shores of Lake Victoria The lake and wetlands are an important source of economic activity for the city, particularly through fishing. The city's residents rely on the fish from Lake Victoria as a primary source of protein, and the fishing industry provides employment for many. Additionally, Lake Victoria supports other economic activities such as transportation and tourism. The Kampala Wetlands also support agriculture and beekeeping, providing another source of income for the city. Overall, the water economy is a critical aspect of Kampala and the wider region.

KAMPALA
Uganda

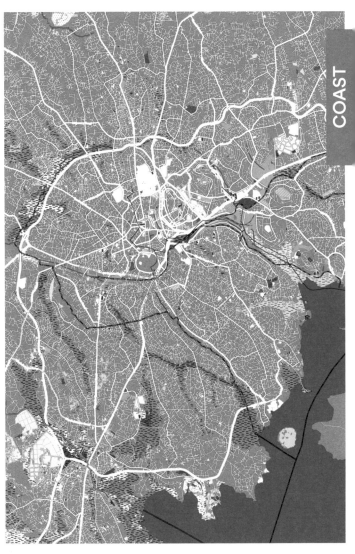

In 2021, Uganda had one of the fastest urban population growth rates in Africa. From 2020-2021, the country also experienced more storms and wet mass movements than most countries on the continent.

1.4m
city population 2022

5.3%
urban population growth rate 2021

$0.71
bottled water

74
floods, storms & wet mass movements 2020-2021

Located in the southwestern part of the country, Kinshasa is the capital and largest city in the Democratic Republic of the Congo. The Congo River is the main water body that flows through Kinshasa. The river is the second-longest river in Africa and the second-largest in the world by discharge volume. The Congo River is one of the most important commercial waterways in Africa. It flows through several countries in Central Africa, connecting Kinshasa with other cities and countries along its course and providing water for drinking, irrigation, fishing, transportation, and hydroelectric power generation. There are also several smaller tributaries, streams and lakes in and around Kinshasa although pollution and environmental degradation are significant challenges for the sustainable development of the city and the well-being of its residents.

KINSHASA
Democratic Republic of the Congo

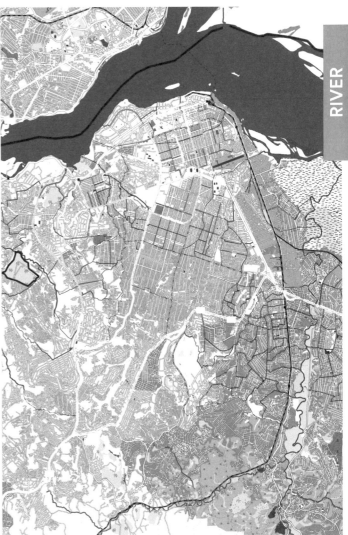

The Democratic Republic of the Congo has a high birth rate. In 2021, the DRC had the lowest GDP per capita and perceived highest levels of corruption correlating with the largest internal displacements caused by conflict on the continent.

3.7m
city population 2022

5.3m
internally displaced persons due to conflict in 2020-2021

$1.08
bottled water

42
births per 1,000 people 2021

Lagos, the largest city in Nigeria, is located in the southwestern part of Nigeria, on the Atlantic Ocean coast. The city is known for having several creeks, which are narrow waterways that flow into the Lagos Lagoon and ultimately the Atlantic Ocean. These creeks are not only important for the economy of Lagos but also provide habitats for aquatic life and serve as important water sources for nearby communities. The lagoon plays a crucial role in the city's economy and is an important transportation link, connecting the city's islands and mainland through a network of bridges and ferry services. The lagoon is also a major commercial hub, with a bustling port that serves as the gateway to Lagos and the surrounding region.

LAGOS
Nigeria

LAGOON

Lagos is the most populous city in Africa. Nigeria's population is highly exposed to flooding and in 2020-2021 the country suffered more floods, storms and wet mass movements than most countries in Africa.

Libreville, the capital city of Gabon, is located on the coast of the Atlantic Ocean and connected to several waterways. The main waterway in Libreville is the Gabon Estuary, which flows into the Atlantic Ocean. The estuary is formed by the convergence of several rivers, including the Komo River, which flows through the city. The estuary and the river are important for the city's economy and daily life. The port of Libreville is an important commercial hub, with many goods being shipped in and out of the city via the river and the ocean. The river is also an important source of water for the city, and it is used for irrigation and hydroelectric power generation. Libreville's waterways are an important part of the city's infrastructure and economy, and contribute to its natural beauty and recreational opportunities.

LIBREVILLE
Gabon

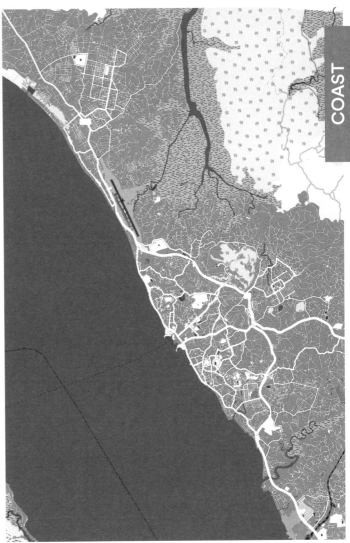

In 2020, Gabon had the largest share of forest cover in Africa. Gabon also has the largest share of urban dwellers on the continent, relative to the country's total population.

0.6m
city population 2022

90%
pop live in urban areas 2020

$1.08
bottled water

91%
land covered by forest 2020

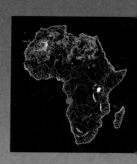

The city of Luanda in Angola is located on the Atlantic coast. The city is an important port, with a deepwater harbour that allows for the shipment of goods in and out of the country. The city's surface water is mainly sourced from the Kwanza River, which is the longest river in Angola and provides water for domestic, industrial, and agricultural use. Luanda has several bays in and around the city, the main one being the Bay of Luanda, which is a large natural harbour located just west of the city. Another bay located near Luanda is the large Mussulo Bay, which is located to the south of the city. Mussulo Bay is known for its sandy beaches and clear waters and is a popular destination for swimming, sunbathing, and water sports.

LUANDA
Angola

In 2020, Angola had one of the highest rates of inflation on the continent. In 2021, Angola's birth rate was one of the highest of the continent and the country's urban population grew faster than the continental average. Angola does have one of the lowest levels of water stress.

2.8m
city population
2022

18%
annual inflation GDP
deflector 2020

$2.28
bottled water

39
births per 1,000
people 2021

Monrovia is the capital city of Liberia located on the west coast of Africa. The city has several sources of surface water. The most significant river in Monrovia is the St. Paul River. This is the longest river in Liberia and flows through the city before emptying into the Atlantic Ocean. It is a major source of water for the city, providing water for irrigation, transportation, and domestic use. Other rivers that flow through Monrovia include the Mesurado and Du rivers. The Mesurado River flows through the heart of Monrovia and is an important landmark in the city. The river serves as a natural boundary between the two largest neighbourhoods in Monrovia, namely Sinkor and Central Monrovia. It is also an important economic and cultural resource for the region and it is likely to be an important factor in the city's development and growth.

MONROVIA
Liberia

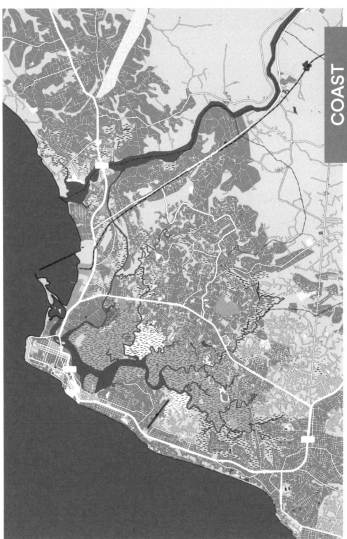

COAST

In 2020, Liberia's income from natural resources and share of land covered by forest was one of the highest in Africa. The country's high levels of rainfall contribute to its notably low level of water stress. However, the country's GDP per ppp was one of the lowest in Africa in 2021.

0.9m
city population 2022

79%
land covered by forest

$1.32
1.5 L water

0.3%
water stress 2019

Port Louis is the capital city of Mauritius. The port of Port Louis is the main port of the city and the largest harbour in Mauritius. It is a natural harbour, home to many fishing boats and shipping vessels and is one of the busiest in the Indian Ocean, handling goods from around the world. The ocean also supports a thriving fishing industry, with seafood being a staple of the local cuisine. Caudan Waterfront, built on reclaimed land, is a popular shopping and entertainment complex, marina and a promenade located on the waterfront in Port Louis. Additionally, the city's beaches attract tourists who enjoy water-based activities such as swimming, surfing, and snorkeling. The relationship between Port Louis and the ocean highlights the need to sustainably ensure the continued health of the marine ecosystem and its economic benefits.

PORT LOUIS
Mauritius

In 2020, Mauritius had the highest net foreign direct investment on the continent. In 2021, Mauritius had the lowest birth rate and lowest urban population growth in Africa, whilst having the highest population density.

0.2m
city population 2022

624
people per sq/km 2021

$0.57
1.5 L water

12.7B
FDI (net) 2020

Victoria is the capital city of the Republic of Seychelles, an island nation located in the Indian Ocean. It is situated on the island of Mahe, which is the largest and most populous island in the Seychelles archipelago. Including the Indian Ocean, Victoria is surrounded by several major water bodies, such as the Sainte Anne Marine National Park. These water bodies play a crucial role in the city's economy, particularly through tourism. The crystal-clear waters and white sandy beaches attract visitors from around the world, and water-based activities such as scuba diving, snorkeling, and boat tours are popular among tourists. The fishing industry is also an important source of income for the city, with the waters surrounding Seychelles home to a variety of fish and seafood.

VICTORIA
Seychelles

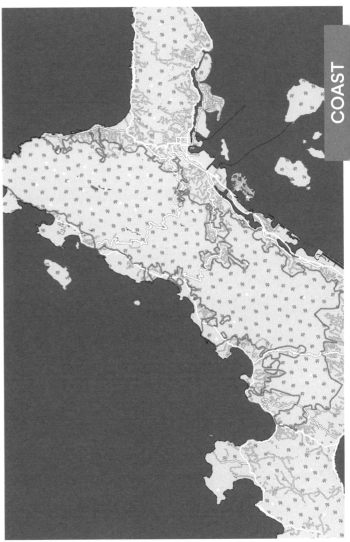

In 2019, Seychelles experienced some of the highest rainfall in Africa and its transportation sector was the second largest emitter of CO_2 per capita on the continent, excluding aviation and shipping. In 2021, the country was considered to have the lowest level of corruption on the continent.

0.2m
city population 2022

70/100
corruption score 2021

$1.03
bottled water

$27k
GDP per capita ppp 2021

RANK	COUNTRY	CITY	Crude Birth Rate (per 1,000 people) 2021	Population Density (people per sq/km) 2021	Urban Population Growth (annual %) 2021	Urban Population, Most Populous City per Country 2021	GDP per capita (PPP US$) 2021	Economic Growth, Change of Real GDP (Average Annual %) 2005-2020	Inflation, GDP Deflator (annual %) 2020	Foreign Direct Investment, net (BoP, current US$) 2020	Corruption, Perceived Least Corrupt Public Sector (index /100) 2021	Internal Displacement Caused by Conflict 2021	Gender Equality (index /r) 2021	Covid-19 Containment and Health, Government Response Stringency (index /100) 2022
1	Nigeria	Lagos	81,95	37,18	72,73	100,00	18,30	44,57	1,41	-7,16	34,29	60,46	78,79	36,97
2	Congo DRC	Kinshasa	92,84	6,57	80,00	23,90	4,08	57,66	0,70	-11,76	27,14	100,00	70,90	61,61
3	Mauritius	Port Louis	22,84	100,00	1,82	1,01	74,54	27,41	0,25	100,00	77,14	-	83,72	41,08
4	Angola	Luanda	85,68	4,33	74,55	18,04	22,06	44,37	3,23	15,37	41,43	-	78,67	47,62
5	Ghana	Accra	60,82	22,28	58,18	12,76	20,71	62,74	1,68	-10,47	61,43	-	82,86	64,75
6	Ethiopia	Addis Ababa	71,50	16,67	85,45	17,92	8,71	100,00	3,27	-18,81	55,71	67,22	87,55	62,65
7	Morocco	Casablanca	38,74	13,46	36,36	20,44	27,29	33,71	0,15	-7,53	55,71	-	76,94	61,02
8	Benin	Cotonou	80,82	17,63	54,55	5,07	12,70	44,77	0,52	-1,20	60,00	0,05	75,46	39,03
9	Egypt	Cairo	49,80	16,83	36,36	50,26	44,63	45,58	1,11	-43,39	47,14	-	78,30	51,47
10	South Africa	Cape Town	43,76	7,85	36,36	22,31	48,33	18,17	0,94	-39,97	62,86	-	96,42	36,97
11	Liberia	Monrovia	69,08	8,65	60,00	6,11	5,20	40,30	-1,00	-	41,43	-	87,42	75,81
12	Congo	Brazzaville	67,76	2,72	58,18	8,35	12,12	16,04	-2,48	7,87	30,00	1,07	-	40,04
13	Gabon	Libreville	59,93	1,44	49,09	3,76	52,27	26,29	-1,64	-	44,29	-	-	31,83
14	Cameroon	Douala	77,14	9,29	63,64	8,70	13,62	37,46	0,10	-4,64	38,57	17,03	85,33	25,67
15	Uganda	Kampala	81,24	37,66	96,36	8,79	8,04	61,83	0,49	-6,86	38,57	0,03	89,27	70,36
16	Côte d'Ivoire	Abidjan	74,92	13,62	61,82	50,60	19,91	50,25	0,17	-5,59	51,43	5,66	77,93	46,22
17	Seychelles	Victoria	34,07	34,62	27,27	0,15	100,00	41,42	-0,54	-1,06	100,00	-	-	40,04
18	Senegal	Dakar	71,92	14,26	67,27	16,09	12,63	41,62	0,27	-	61,43	0,16	82,37	61,21
19	Algeria	Algiers	47,52	3,04	43,64	12,85	40,34	23,25	-0,99	-8,87	47,14	-	74,23	46,22
20	Sierra Leone	Freetown	69,24	18,11	56,36	5,22	6,09	46,90	1,95	-1,06	48,57	0,10	82,86	77,23
21	Zimbabwe	Harare	67,42	6,25	30,91	10,03	8,19	22,94	100,00	-1,21	32,86	-	90,51	100,00
22	Togo	Lomé	70,33	25,00	67,27	4,87	7,98	41,42	0,23	-0,42	42,86	-	85,94	75,50
23	Rwanda	Kigali	66,18	86,22	60,00	7,36	8,36	71,07	1,20	-1,20	75,71	-	100,00	65,41
24	Tunisia	Tunis	35,53	12,34	25,45	4,50	38,86	20,91	1,23	-4,65	62,86	-	79,28	68,67
25	Libya	Tripoli	39,36	0,64	29,09	7,48	78,28	14,92	-0,91	2,75	24,29	3,00	-	33,89
26	Kenya	Nairobi	61,12	15,54	72,73	17,87	16,84	46,19	0,88	-4,47	42,86	3,56	89,89	46,83
27	Zambia	Lusaka	76,19	4,01	74,55	8,24	12,15	54,92	2,46	-1,42	47,14	-	89,15	34,92
28	Gambia	Banjul	73,43	39,42	70,91	2,98	8,16	26,40	0,72	-1,52	52,86	-	79,04	46,22
29	São Tomé and Príncipe	São Tomé	62,40	37,34	52,73	0,35	14,90	48,12	0,98	-0,36	64,29	-	-	-
30	Guinea	Conakry	76,01	8,81	69,09	11,48	9,65	50,46	0,88	-1,37	35,71	-	79,78	59,02
31	Mali	Bamako	91,94	2,72	85,45	3,52	8,20	42,44	0,10	-4,21	41,43	6,11	74,11	54,00
32	Burkina Faso	Ouagadougou	78,47	12,66	87,27	7,06	8,25	56,95	1,22	0,72	60,00	29,59	81,26	43,13
33	Mozambique	Maputo	80,80	6,57	78,18	7,74	4,50	58,38	0,45	-23,83	37,14	13,77	92,73	35,94
34	Chad	Ndjamena	95,73	2,08	72,73	4,69	5,33	38,78	-0,98	-	28,57	7,34	71,39	41,08
35	Sudan	Khartoum	74,17	3,85	58,18	12,83	14,13	4,37	20,64	-5,63	28,57	59,47	-	18,48
36	Equatorial Guinea	Bata	67,33	8,33	70,91	1,12	60,75	13,60	-1,58	-	24,29	-	-	-
37	Burundi	Bujumbura	76,93	76,44	100,00	2,16	2,66	25,99	1,97	-	27,14	0,36	95,81	57,51
38	Botswana	Gaborone	52,05	0,64	52,73	1,35	22,18	36,95	0,78	-0,79	78,57	-	88,66	24,65
39	Malawi	Lilongwe	72,55	33,33	76,36	4,20	5,56	49,44	1,83	-1,56	50,00	-	77,93	79,07
40	Tanzania	Dar es Salaam	79,95	11,06	90,91	17,54	9,83	51,27	0,06	-5,38	55,71	-	88,66	19,51
41	Niger	Niamey	100,00	3,21	81,82	5,03	4,39	57,97	0,16	-2,71	44,29	4,20	78,30	34,30
42	Mauritania	Nouakchott	73,29	0,80	74,55	4,30	18,74	41,73	0,63	-7,29	40,00	-	-	36,97
43	Somalia	Mogadishu	96,18	4,17	76,36	16,81	4,37	74,82	1,41	-	18,57	55,59	-	28,76
44	Madagascar	Antananarivo	68,33	7,85	80,00	9,04	5,48	25,99	0,91	-1,88	37,14	0,05	90,63	19,51
45	Comoros	Moroni	64,91	76,44	52,73	0,36	11,01	28,22	0,12	-0,03	28,57	-	77,81	-
46	Cape Verde	Praia	37,43	22,28	30,91	0,74	23,55	30,56	-0,15	-0,33	82,86	-	90,75	43,13
47	Guinea-Bissau	Bissau	68,64	11,54	60,00	2,52	6,89	33,81	0,02	-0,16	30,00	-	-	-
48	Namibia	Windhoek	60,58	0,48	67,27	1,74	32,86	26,29	0,74	1,65	70,00	-	99,51	30,81
49	Central African Republic	Bangui	94,23	1,28	52,73	8,43	3,42	12,59	0,35	-	34,29	12,96	-	43,13
50	Lesotho	Maseru	57,64	11,38	41,82	0,77	8,99	21,54	2,35	-0,22	54,29	-	86,31	40,04
51	Swaziland	Mbabane	53,28	10,90	34,55	0,62	32,90	27,61	0,65	-0,40	45,71	-	89,77	36,97
52	Djibouti	Djibouti	49,03	6,89	29,09	4,05	19,86	56,14	0,32	-1,24	42,86	-	-	33,89
53	South Sudan	Juba	64,26	3,85	58,18	2,92	6,18	-49,95	-	-	15,71	25,64	-	37,37
54	Eritrea	Asmara	63,20	5,77	54,55	3,66	7,74	11,57	-	-	31,43	-	-	-

Highest   Median   Lowest

INFRASTRUCTURE				MORPHOLOGY				ENVIRONMENT				RESOURCES				TOTAL
Container Port Traffic (20 foot equivalent units) 2020	Logistics Performance, Quality of Trade and Transport-Related Infrastructure Index /5) 2018	Individuals using the Internet (% of population) 2020	CO$_2$ Emissions from Transport (tonnes of CO$_2$e per capita) 2019	Population Living in Slums (% of urban population) 2020	Population Living in Urban Areas (% of population) 2020 /100	Access to Electricity (% of population) 2020/100	Elevation Above Sea Level, Most Populous City per Country (m) /100	Annual Precipitation (mm per year) 2019	Internal Displacements Caused By Floods & Storms 2020–2021 /100	Population Exposed to Flooding 2022 /100	Flood & Storm Disaster Events 2020–2021/100	Income from natural resources, (% of GDP) 2020 /100	Land Covered by Forest (% of land area) 2020 /100	Water Stress (% of freshwater withdrawal compared to avaiable freshwater sources) 2019 /100	Agricultural Raw Material Exports (% of merchandise exports) 2017–2021 /100	28 INDEXES / 2800
21,90	80,25	42,20	11,10	59,73	57,67	55,40	99,66	35,94	14,45	93,02	100,00	19,22	25,96	1,18	0,35	1277,5
0,60	66,46	16,17	1,01	95,56	50,66	19,10	81,62	48,22	25,50	87,21	43,24	22,58	60,90	0,03	0,81	1133,3
6,28	87,77	77,13	37,72	-	45,24	99,66	99,74	63,78	0,01	1,16	2,70	0,00	20,92	2,65	0,80	1075,4
9,63	58,31	42,80	9,95	76,34	74,17	46,89	99,74	31,56	1,40	59,30	14,86	54,71	58,49	0,23	0,00	1073,7
15,05	76,49	68,95	11,17	40,84	63,66	85,87	97,64	37,09	0,53	56,98	9,46	16,27	38,44	0,77	1,47	1058,4
-	-	28,53	2,75	78,43	24,08	51,09	1,59	26,50	100,00	66,28	72,97	9,15	16,54	3,95	13,31	1053,0
100,00	76,18	100,00	20,79	13,23	70,52	100,00	98,37	10,81	0,02	67,44	2,70	0,67	14,13	6,21	0,87	1038,2
7,32	78,37	30,67	19,99	82,85	53,74	41,41	99,91	32,47	0,81	59,30	4,05	4,24	30,45	0,12	100,00	1035,1
84,92	88,40	85,49	21,45	1,10	47,49	100,00	99,14	0,57	0,45	94,19	2,70	10,40	0,00	17,28	1,92	1033,6
57,71	100,00	83,21	38,96	29,51	74,76	84,39	99,44	15,47	0,51	58,14	14,86	8,23	15,44	7,78	2,28	1024,7
1,31	59,87	30,43	5,58	77,91	57,82	27,53	99,48	74,72	0,18	72,09	4,05	25,97	86,64	0,03	-	1016,6
7,97	64,89	-	9,87	53,88	75,29	49,52	86,69	51,44	27,04	100,00	58,11	100,00	70,43	0,00	18,97	1015,8
2,76	65,52	73,70	3,49	54,02	100,00	91,57	99,14	57,22	0,00	55,81	1,35	43,58	100,00	0,06	-	1015,5
5,67	80,56	44,94	5,00	39,84	63,89	64,72	98,50	50,13	5,58	69,77	4,05	11,55	47,10	0,19	27,05	990,4
-	68,65	7,25	3,17	65,87	27,70	42,07	49,46	36,88	4,15	59,30	100,00	12,78	12,81	0,71	3,24	979,8
13,96	90,60	-	6,58	64,89	57,39	69,68	97,85	42,13	0,08	65,12	1,35	5,18	-	0,62	14,91	977,3
2,21	-	93,91	85,76	-	63,87	100,00	99,31	72,81	0,00	1,16	0,00	0,19	80,28	-	0,00	975,5
8,06	69,59	50,64	7,32	38,54	53,41	70,37	98,50	21,44	0,22	55,81	4,05	2,69	45,89	1,99	1,64	959,4
10,39	75,86	74,77	42,29	16,18	81,84	99,80	98,71	2,78	0,08	60,47	5,41	34,30	0,88	16,88	0,07	949,1
1,12	57,05	21,40	2,30	61,76	47,64	26,20	95,45	78,94	0,00	53,49	0,00	27,60	38,44	0,06	12,60	935,6
-	57,37	34,83	6,98	26,30	35,79	52,75	36,11	20,53	6,38	69,77	56,76	5,22	49,40	4,33	2,90	933,3
24,71	69,91	28,53	5,23	46,95	47,51	54,00	99,70	36,50	0,00	50,00	0,00	6,73	24,32	0,42	10,86	926,3
-	86,52	28,29	-	46,77	19,35	46,60	34,95	37,88	0,36	51,16	9,46	6,64	12,27	2,47	1,75	924,8
6,02	65,83	85,47	24,98	9,32	77,22	100,00	98,02	6,47	0,57	55,81	4,05	4,53	4,93	11,75	0,52	900,5
3,89	70,53	-	100,00	-	89,57	69,71	99,53	1,75	0,06	30,23	2,70	93,25	0,11	100,00	0,04	894,2
18,78	79,94	35,07	7,25	61,97	31,07	71,44	28,51	19,69	17,58	65,12	13,51	2,19	6,90	4,07	19,71	892,6
-	72,10	23,54	4,60	58,85	49,54	44,52	46,20	31,88	0,35	63,95	9,46	13,43	66,05	0,35	0,87	888,0
1,02	57,05	43,39	1,53	47,43	69,46	62,27	99,91	26,13	0,94	40,70	5,41	4,85	26,29	0,27	0,29	885,6
-	73,04	39,23	7,42	64,15	82,53	76,56	93,99	100,00	0,02	1,16	1,35	3,68	59,26	0,23	0,10	883,5
2,83	48,90	30,91	4,78	59,76	40,93	44,67	95,79	51,59	0,24	59,30	5,41	8,59	27,60	0,17	2,35	883,3
-	72,10	32,57	5,71	51,13	48,74	50,56	86,00	8,81	0,64	80,23	4,05	3,74	11,94	0,98	15,96	879,0
-	76,18	26,15	6,56	32,38	33,97	18,96	87,38	23,38	0,94	53,49	1,35	8,75	24,86	0,96	12,03	873,9
6,26	-	19,61	4,82	67,02	41,15	30,60	99,23	32,25	3,26	73,26	8,11	23,63	51,15	0,21	1,77	854,7
-	74,29	12,36	1,98	100,00	26,11	11,08	87,42	10,06	4,53	87,21	21,62	44,12	3,72	0,53	-	851,8
7,06	68,34	33,76	9,84	89,88	39,13	55,39	83,56	7,81	26,30	93,02	8,11	12,20	10,84	14,52	-	848,8
0,14	58,93	-	16,19	-	81,14	66,75	98,63	67,38	-	51,16	-	64,57	95,62	0,02	0,00	845,3
-	61,13	11,17	2,08	44,88	15,22	11,74	66,29	39,81	5,57	43,02	37,84	19,24	11,94	1,25	1,94	840,1
-	-	76,08	41,58	48,29	78,67	71,99	57,23	13,00	0,04	55,81	1,35	1,38	29,46	0,26	0,10	833,0
-	68,34	-	2,53	60,71	19,34	14,87	54,66	36,91	1,40	61,63	16,22	11,30	26,07	2,14	1,21	826,0
5,20	-	26,15	3,39	49,85	39,10	39,90	97,55	33,47	4,93	67,44	17,57	4,26	4,93	1,59	4,60	819,1
-	62,70	-	2,00	85,85	18,45	19,25	90,64	4,72	18,75	86,05	4,05	10,86	0,99	1,35	0,20	816,8
1,21	70,85	48,50	14,38	68,29	61,41	47,35	100,00	2,88	0,07	87,21	1,35	26,76	0,33	1,62	0,01	815,9
1,32	56,74	-	0,39	-	51,22	49,73	97,42	8,81	52,38	87,21	12,16	0,00	10,41	3,00	-	807,8
2,86	67,71	-	2,09	82,22	42,77	33,74	46,37	47,28	1,12	83,72	8,11	7,92	23,44	1,38	2,32	796,1
0,78	70,53	-	8,44	83,66	32,61	86,74	98,88	28,13	0,00	1,16	0,00	2,53	19,39	0,10	0,09	773,2
0,75	-	76,68	21,77	-	73,98	94,16	98,97	7,13	0,04	1,16	2,70	0,65	12,38	1,03	0,00	753,1
0,41	55,80	27,22	2,49	74,16	49,06	33,34	99,01	49,28	0,00	38,37	0,00	17,99	77,11	0,18	-	737,7
2,39	-	48,74	32,64	-	57,76	56,26	29,07	8,91	0,02	70,93	2,70	2,44	8,87	0,11	2,73	715,5
-	60,50	12,36	1,77	-	46,84	15,47	83,90	41,97	1,83	66,28	27,03	17,44	39,21	0,04	25,37	703,4
-	61,44	51,12	10,52	31,16	32,22	47,35	33,71	24,63	0,03	34,88	1,35	6,37	1,20	0,31	8,61	669,3
-	-	-	21,55	13,18	26,83	79,73	48,99	24,63	-	48,84	-	6,20	31,65	9,49	8,78	652,4
11,64	87,46	70,14	6,15	-	86,65	61,77	44,44	6,88	0,00	4,65	1,35	0,61	0,33	0,78	-	623,7
6,16	-	7,73	2,99	-	22,42	7,24	79,09	28,13	45,15	82,56	58,11	12,20	12,38	0,52	-	528,8
0,39	58,31	-	2,97	-	-	52,17	0,00	12,00	0,00	36,05	1,35	0,00	11,39	1,37	-	353,9

TOP 20 AFRICAN WATER CITIES

WATER CITIES
PROJECT ATLAS

Title: Makoko Water Cities | Medium: Photo Collage | Year: 2014 | Architect: NLÉ with Iwan Baan photography

'Over 70% of Africa's major cities and capitals are by water.'

Water Cities Project Atlas

Legend — Infrastructure Types

 Water Transportation
 Canalization
 Dike Construction
 Flood Basins
 Floating Structures
 Storm Barriers
Land Reclamation
 Wetlands
Permeable Pavement
 Slope Embankment
Green Roofs

Waterbodies

- Coast
- River
- Lagoon
- Lake
- Floodplain
- Surface
- Wetlands

Water Cities Project Atlas

1. Floating Building Systems, Cabo Verde
2. Land Reclamation, Seychelles
3. Shoreline Defense, Senegal
4. Mangrove Restoration, Kenya
5. Flood Relief Channel, Eswatini
6. Stilt Buildings, South Africa
7. River Revitalization, Algeria
8. River Catchment, Rwanda
9. Urban Rehabilitation, Benon
10. Basin Control, Burkina Faso
11. Hybrid Hydro-Solar Plant, Ghana
12. Drainage Lake, Togo
13. Flood Control Dredging, Ghana
14. Water Transportation, Nigeria
15. Stilt Infrastructure, Liberia
16. Incremental Reclamation, Abidjan
17. Dike Networks, South Sudan
18. Community Preparedness, Sudan, Niger, Burkina Faso
19. Vernacular Mounds, Namibia
20. Levees, Mali
21. Urban Wetlands, Rwanda
22. Drainage Restoration, Tanzania
23. Water Harvesting, Tanzania
24. Vegetation Control, South Africa

WATER CITIES PROJECT ATLAS

Adaptation & Mitigation

The **Water Cities Atlas** is a knowledge platform to bring local intelligence of water cities, communities, and global solutions into a collective by identifying, gathering and cultivating various projects and initiatives being undertaken in different regions, showing adaptation and mitigation measures at various scales. The basis of this platform are two big trends of our time: urbanization by population growth — Africa will grow from 1.1 billion people today to 3.44 billion[1], and a changing climate, as even if emissions are minimized, sea levels are expected to rise by an approximate 0.3 to 0.6 metres by 2100.[2]

Overlap of the phenomena of rapid urbanization and impact of climate change—particularly in Africa as this is the continent where these trends are manifested most extremely—can instigate urban innovation. It is the rapidly growing and increasingly climate change-impacted cities that may generate the responsible solutions for development.

To amplify this, because flood-prone or inundated areas are often the most affordable land (or water), migration causes these areas to urbanize at a relatively fast rate[9]. It is these conditions that we have found to be at the forefront of adaptation, finding new forms of building and living—with and on water.

Projects

This chapter categorizes projects in six types of water bodies: coast, river, lake, lagoon, floodplain, and surface. These different water bodies have unique ecologies, which are impacted differently by climate and environmental conditions such as storms, heavy rainfall, sea level rise and flooding.

In the research, we find places such as the Cuvai basin, a unique area within south-west Africa. It is a floodplain that once per year transforms from dry desert to an inundated series of channels and lakes; a desert water world. The four big urban areas are urbanizing at about five per cent per year, with 84 per cent of the total population still living in rural areas.[4] While there is a vernacular solution to the yearly occurring flood rains—building on mounds—in these fast-growing cities the area of higher grounds is not always big enough. To mitigate this, Ondjiva, a city of 55,000 people, has implemented a series of stormwater dikes[5] that aim to protect its populated areas while minimizing the disruption of the annual flow of water.

Another example is the coast of Cote D'Ivoire in Abidjan, a coastal metropolis of over five million inhabitants, large parts of which are situated less than a metre above sea level.[7] Much of its historic mangrove forests and wetlands have been sand-filled. Both formally, by adding to port and industrial areas and waterfront high-end residential developments (as much as 119 ha[6]), as well as informally, now housing tens of thousands in neighbourhoods such as Soweto Remblais, named after the French proverb of 'reblayer'—to fill something up.

Then there is Ganvie, the renowned water community built in the lake of Nokoué in Benin. Over 80,000 inhabitants live on water, with boats being the only form of urban mobility.

Recognizing its potential as affordable urban development with minimal impact to the environment and economic potential for tourism, there is a local initiative to renovate much of the low-carbon timber stilt housing, as well as implement jetties and other improvements to infrastructures bridging land to water. Residents have historically migrated to other water-based communities along the West-African coast, including Makoko.

In development since 2011, and in close collaboration with builders, communities, governments, engineers, and artists, the Makoko Floating System is a prefabricated self-build floating building solution that can be adapted for various uses. The iconic structure—a 60 degree triangle in elevation—is an ideal form for tall floating structures as the building geometry's low centre of gravity gives it greater stability and balance. It is designed to be assembled with modular timber beams, without the need for heavy machinery or equipment. Floating on a modular foundation, the low-carbon building system can adapt to changing water levels while minimizing its impact on the water and ecological conditions below.

The projects included in this chapter are just some of the many potential solutions for the development and urban regeneration of both their own and other waterfronts. African cities and communities are implementing and developing a wide range of climate adaptation and mitigation strategies, in a maelstrom of existing and growing urban areas. The projects are wide ranging: architectural, social, infrastructural, environmental, vernacular, and so on. These interventions in urban adaptation are not always perfect and come with learnings and failures, advantages and disadvantages, in pursuit of inclusive development and new forms of urbanism.

The Water Cities Project Atlas as a knowledge platform will continue to bring these interventions, efforts and projects together with an aim to share and develop socially inclusive, resilient and ecologically intelligent solutions for the future.

'Makoko Floating System (MFS™) is a simple way to build on water by hand.'

MFS™ is a modular, scalable and affordable prefabricated floating building system for sustainable and inclusive developments of waterfronts. MFS™ is available in three sizes, small, medium and large vessels. The three sizes range from one to three floors and are available in different internal floor configurations to create floating cottages, lofts or large performance spaces. MFS™ provides an alternative approach to development through the use of lightweight timber structures that float on water. Constructed from low-carbon renewable materials, mainly wood or bamboo, steel connections and floaters, MFS™ is a low-tech structural frame that can be fitted with relevant hi-tech equipment. MFS™ provides inclusive employment for local residents, through low skill labour with simple hand tools, as well as a building block for city builders of emerging opportunities.

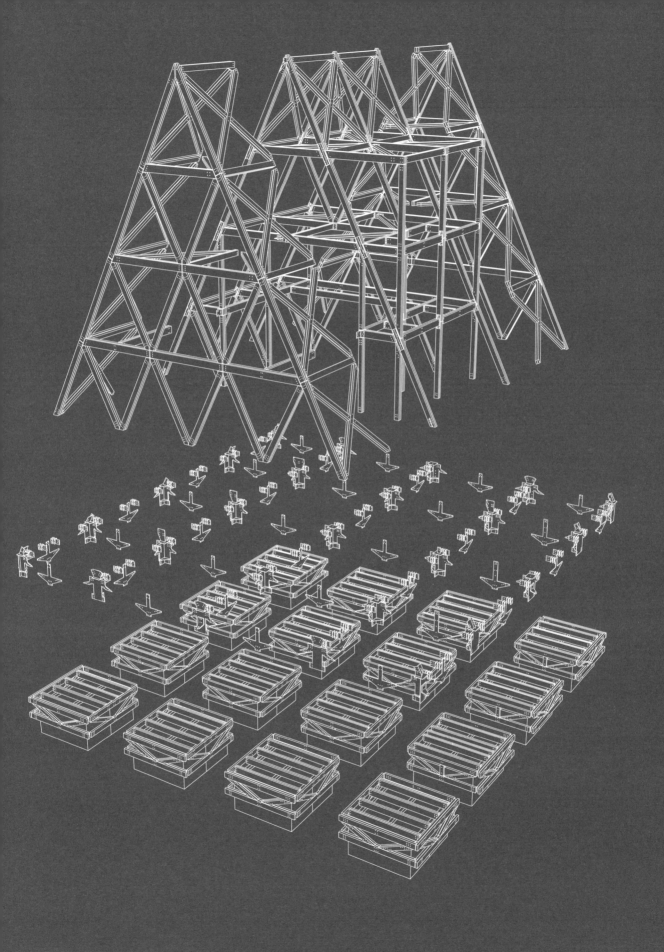

MFS IV under construction in Mindelo Harbor, Cabo Verde

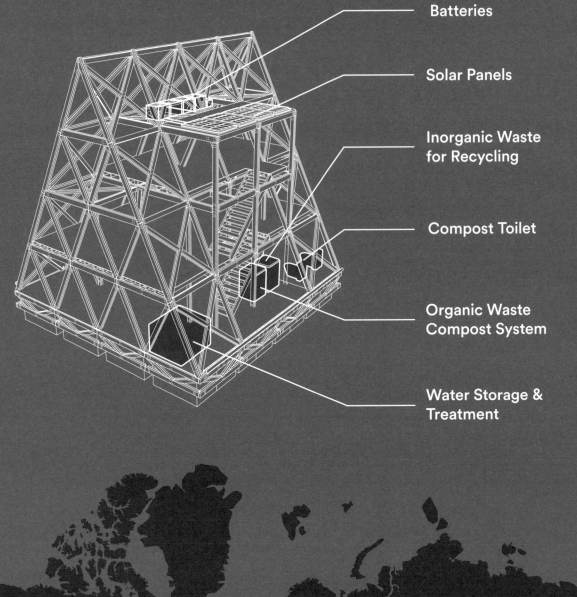

Batteries

Solar Panels

Inorganic Waste
for Recycling

Compost Toilet

Organic Waste
Compost System

Water Storage &
Treatment

MFS has been deployed in 6 countries on 3 continents in various climatic conditions and
water bodies including a lagoon, lakes and an ocean coast, demonstrating its potential for
regional adaptation and versatility.

Lagos, Nigeria 2012 Makoko Floating School

Venice, Italy 2016 MFSII

Bruges, Belgium 2018 MFSIII, Macarthur Floating School

Chengdu, China 2018 MFSIVx3

Mindelo, Cabo Verde 2020 MFS IV

WATER CITIES PROJECT ATLAS

FLOATING BUILDINGS

Floating Music Hub
Mindelo, Cabo Verde, 2021

The Floating Music Hub, Mindelo (Mansa Floating Hub), is a cultural and creative platform located in the beautiful bay of Mindelo, on the island of São Vicente, Cape Verde, West Africa. The platform is based on NLÉ's innovative floating building solution called Makoko Floating System (MFS™), a simple way to build on water using lightweight, prefabricated, modular timber elements that can be easily assembled and disassembled.

Floating buildings are one potential solution to urbanizing flood prone or inundated areas in a climate-resilient and ecologically conscious way.

LAND RECLAMATION

Ile Perseverance
Mahé, Seychelles, 2002-present

Seychelles has relatively little suitable land for
development, which makes urban expansion on
Mahé restricted. Land reclamation projects such as
Perseverance Island aim to relieve land pressures
by expanding onto water.

With land on the island becoming increasingly
scarce, the government of Seychelles has
undertaken reclamation works since the 1970s.
Land is predominantly occupied by housing, which
is replacing some of the former agricultural land.

SHORELINE DEFENSE

Saint Louis Sea Barrier
Saint Louis, Senegal, 2023

The historical city of Saint Louis is registered as a World Heritage Site, located on a sandbar on the northwest coast of Senegal between the Senegal River and Atlantic Ocean. Senegal's fishing communities are threatened and forced inland by storm surges causing high rates of erosion and encroaching the shoreline at an average of 1.8 metres a year.

Riprap walls like those under construction in Saint Louis aim to mitigate the problem of erosion but such measures are unable to provide full protection against the highest waves. Further measures such as breakwaters, a new sea wall or resanding the beaches to create a buffer zone are necessary.

MANGROVE RESTORATION

Mikoko Pamoja
Gazi Bay, Kenya, 2010-ongoing

Mangrove Wetlands cover a small percentage of the Earth's surface, yet they are some of the most valuable environmental resources. Mangrove root systems and the soil they accumulate are essential as natural defences against coastal erosion and storm surges. Along Kenya's long coastline, bays, creeks, and rivers containing mangrove habitats have historically been threatened by degradation caused by deforestation, aquaculture, and fisheries. Mikoko Pamoja in Gazi Bay is considered the world's first blue carbon project. It is one of multiple mangrove restoration projects underway in Kenya. Funding the replanting and maintenance of mangrove habitats is difficult. Hybrid, income-generating schemes like this, incentivize local communities to maintain mangroves and their wider ecosystem through carbon credit and offset projects, ecotourism ventures, and education, amongst others.

FLOOD RELIEF CHANNEL

Sigangeni Stream Restoration
Mbabane, Eswatini, 2005-2012

Interlocking concrete retaining blocks (CRB) aim to offer a minimally invasive, heavy earthworks solution to riparian floods and embankment erosion. By first removing unstable soil, backfilling the landscape and connecting the blockwork system to drainage solutions such as wick drains, the flow of the river can be controlled and excess water drained out of porous soil, reducing the risk of surface water build-up. The growth of vegetation further reinforces the vertical blockwork system.

Thesen Islands Redevelopment
Knysna, South Africa, 2000-2008

Thesen Island was a timber treatment facility in the 1920s. The Knysna Estuary is considered one of the most sensitive and biodiverse ecosystems in South Africa. Therefore, after the facility was closed in 1990, the islands were sensitively redeveloped and environmentally rehabilitated to become a community consisting of over 500 vernacular style, timber homes across 19 man-made islands. Now, the estuary is particularly attractive to tourism.

Nature-based developments such as this aim to uphold strict planning conditions to ensure the area remains attractive to both residents and wildlife, as well as visitors.

RIVER REVITALIZATION

Oued El-Harrach Ecological Corridor
Algiers, Algeria, 2009-2029 (est.)

For a considerable period, the El Harrach River has suffered from extensive pollution, 30 times the expected standard and exceeding WHO standards by 400 times. The river passes through a crucial urban and industrial zone for its final nine kilometres to its outfall into the Mediterranean Sea. Efforts are underway to rejuvenate the river by dividing it into five segments, positioning it as green heritage and a catalyst for the city of tomorrow.

Redevelopment and restoration of rivers like these, aims to focus on the protection of ecosystems and their potential to serve as a channel for urbanization in the medium and long term.

RIVER CATCHMENT

Nyabarongo River Catchment Plan
Kigali, Rwanda, 2018-2024 (est.)

Interventions such as The Nyabarongo Catchment Area Plan in Kigali, Rwanda, are created to better manage surface run-off whilst mitigating land degradation and water pollution through a combined water management and resource management strategy.

Mobilizing youths to partake in the terrace farming of productive crops is one of the initiatives in the catchment area plan, which aims to reduce soil erosion, enhance soil productivity and mitigate land degradation. Community projects such as this also aim to promote environmentally friendly income generation activities, as well as green jobs in terracing, agroforestry, and buffer zone management.

URBAN REHABILITATION

Reinventing the lakeside city of Ganvie
Ganvie, Benin, 2017-2026 (est.)

Ganvie, a village established on stilts, is located in the middle of Lake Nokoué, near Cotonou, southern Benin. Over several generations, Ganvie's inhabitants have developed a unique lifestyle founded on fishing and water-based activities, but currently, poverty and environmental challenges threaten the continuation of this lifestyle.

To address these challenges, a project was initiated to improve living conditions by rehabilitating 2,500 homes, establishing floating markets, schools, and other infrastructure while increasing the lake's tourism and economic activities on and with water.

AFRICAN WATER CITIES

BASIN CONTROL

Ouagadougou Northern Interchange
Ouagadougou, Burkina Faso, 2015-2018

Ouagadougou, the largest city in Burkina Faso, is growing at an estimated rate of nine per cent per year. The city is in the Sahel region of West Africa, which experiences extremes in climate fluctuations from intense drought to heavy rainfall causing flooding.

The Northern Intersection, located at the heart of Ouagadougou, sits at the interface of two dams. The replacement of the intersection required the construction of two new dams. Dams like these can manage rainwater storms and water levels for the large lakes in the city.

Bui Floating Solar PV
Bui Reservoir, Ghana, 2016

The Bui Dam in Ghana is dependent on the Black Volta River to produce hydropower. To supplement electricity generated by the hydroelectric dam, a 250 MW solar power plant was installed to offer a solution in times of drought.

Floating Solar Farms can be built on any waterbody, thus limiting evaporation and alleviating land use pressures. Floating PVs may also offer better performance as the water offers the potential to keep them cooler.

DRAINAGE LAKE

The 4th Lake
Lomé, Togo, 2016-2018

To enhance the drainage system and mitigate flooding in the north-eastern region of Lomé, the lagoon system was expanded to include a fourth artificial lake covering 30 hectares, situated in the neighbouring wetlands. The new lake is one of four in Lomé's lagoon network. The lake serves a dual purpose, as both a drainage system for the adjacent wetlands and also collecting rainwater from the surrounding area. Connected to the lake is an open drainage system that will discharge excess water from the lake into the sea.

Improving the efficiency of drainage through lakes like these can improve living conditions and sanitation for the inhabitants of the area.

Korle Lagoon Dredging
Ghana, 2016-2018

Korle Lagoon in Accra is one of the largest in Ghana. The Odaw River flows through the city of Accra, before entering Korle Lagoon and discharging into the Atlantic Ocean. The lagoon has therefore become one of the most polluted water bodies in Ghana and serves as a drainage point for several communities in the Accra Metropolitan Area. As influx of untreated waste into the lagoon is consistent, the river and lagoon have become heavily inundated with refuse, silt and debris causing poor waterflow and flooding during seasonally heavy rainfall.

Although informal settlements along the river and lagoon have made access difficult, routine dredging is considered necessary to avert heavy seasonal rains and storm water from blocking the urban drainage systems persistently threatening human life and the environment.

Lagos State Waterway Authority
Lagos, Nigeria, 2008-ongoing

LASWA regulates and encourages the use of Lagos' waterways. Water transportation is thought to play an important role in the development of Lagos' intermodal transport system. Approximately 17 per cent of Lagos is made up of lagoons and waterways, making the physical environment well-suited to accommodate water mobility services.

Water transportation benefits from larger load capacities, and lower maintenance and operational costs, compared to road or rail. It is considered to have a lower carbon footprint and may also provide faster transport times, particularly in regions with heavy traffic or poor road infrastructure.

Doe Community Approach to Mobility
Monrovia, Liberia, ongoing

Due to population growth and internal migration, informal settlements in low-lying zones of the coastal city of Monrovia have rapidly expanded. The location of these settlements, on swampy, flood-prone land, coupled with frequent, heavy rainfall poses significant risks to the health and livelihood of residents. This has led to communities building elevated walkways and paths to adapt to rising water levels.

Soweto Remblais quarter
Abidjan, Côte D'Ivoire

The densely populated Soweto Remblais quarter in Abidjan takes its name from the French verb *remblayer* which means 'to fill'. By the 1980s, due to more urbanization and evictions, building plots along Abidjan's lagoon front became scarce. This led to new residents and private players incrementally reclaiming the mangrove swamp. Although Soweto Remblais developed outside of state permission and has significant ecological and socio-legal implications, vernacular solutions such as this provide an opportunity to create building land and housing. Over time, the quarter became formally recognized and it received funding to improve road infrastructure from the World Bank.

DIKE NETWORKS

UN Protection of Civilians (PoC) sites
Bentiu, South Sudan, 2013-ongoing

In the Capital of Unity State, South Sudan, UN Protection of Civilians (PoC) sites in Bentiu were established for those displaced by a combination of conflict and flooding. Since then, a network of dikes has been erected by the UN and inhabitants providing an effective adaptation solution to managing water flows and improving drainage. In 2022, floodwaters turned the city and surrounding communities into an island, rendering all roads impassable. Boats and the airstrip became the only means of transportation for delivering aid to the 460,000 individuals residing in the UN Internally Displaced Persons camp. Sandbags continue to provide further temporary solutions to areas where the defence had been breached.

COMMUNITY PREPAREDNESS

Early Warning Systems
Sudan, Senegal, Niger, Burkina Faso, 2022

Countries in Africa's Sahel region can experience sudden meteorological extremes. National meteorological centres in Sudan, Senegal, Niger and Burkina Faso collaborate with climate experts at NORCAP (Norwegian Capacity) to enhance weather forecasting systems and fill resource and data gaps. The 'impact-based forecasting' approaches combine data on hazards, risks and vulnerability to predict what the weather will do, rather than solely what it will be. The objective is to guarantee that high-quality weather and climate forecasts can be communicated and disseminated in a timely and effective way. This aims to empower communities to prepare and save both lives and livelihoods.

MOUNDS

Cuvelai River Basin Vernacular Mounds
Namibia

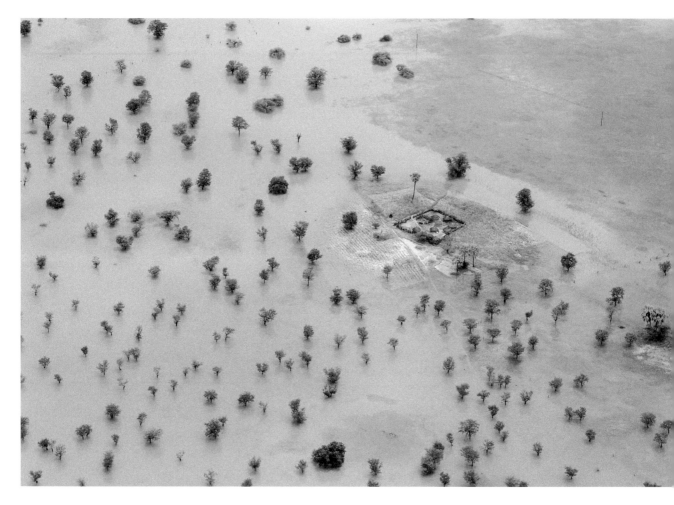

The Cuvelai Basin is a wetland area spanning nearly
160,000 km2, shared by Angola and Namibia. The
basin comprises hundreds of shallow drainage
channels, referred to as iishana, many of which
are dry for most of the year but prone to extensive
flooding during the rainy season, due to the flatness
of the terrain. Between the drainage channels
are mounds of elevated soil. These are used for
housing, crops and livestock and offer an indigenous
adaptation strategy to living in these seasonal
wetlands.

LEVEES

Mopti Levee
Mopti, Mali, 2014-2016

Every year, the discharge of the river Niger
increases several metres during the rainy season.
This causes flooding in large parts of the regional
town of Mopti, 600 km north of the capital Bamako.
A 4.1 km long levee was constructed out of laterite,
aiming to protect the eastern side of the town from
further damage.

URBAN WETLANDS

Nyandungu Eco-Park
Kigali, Rwanda, 2016-2022

The expansion of Kigali has exerted substantial strain on local natural habitats and infringed on Nyandungu urban wetland. Encroachment into the wetlands has led to degradation and loss of biodiversity, whilst also causing flooding downstream and heightened pollution from sewage discharge.

Under the Ministry of Environment, the Rwanda Environment Management Authority (REMA) formulated the Nyandungu Urban Wetland Ecotourism Project and Eco Park in 2016 to transform the wetlands into a recreational park to educate visitors, test and exhibit scalable green technologies in action to curb pollution and mitigate flood hazards in urban regions and restore the wetland ecosystem.

DRAINAGE RESTORATION

Tanzania Urban Resilience Program
Dar es Salaam, Tanzania, 2016-ongoing

The Tanzania Urban Resilience Program (TURP) is a
three-pillar programme of identifying risks through
data collection, risk reduction strategies, and
emergency management. Through the Resilience
Academy, students are given tools to map and
model climate risk and contribute knowledge to
a Climate Risk Database. The aim of participatory
projects like this is to bridge Africa's information,
resilient urban planning and infrastructure gap as
well as mitigate chronic flooding in urban centres
such as Dar es Salaam. These data also helped
to improve solid waste management plans and
drainage infrastructure, and supported local
action of over 100 clean-up activities with 26,000
participants, cleaning 500,000 kg of waste during
the World Clean-up Day Campaign.

WATER HARVESTING

Kariakoo Market
Dar Es Salaam, Tanzania, 1974

Kariakoo market was built in 1974 in the Ilala District of Dar es Salaam, Tanzania. Trading in the Kariakoo ward now extends several city blocks and plays a significant role in Dar es Salaam's food provision and small-scale economy. The Kariakoo Market building in the ward's centre was designed to be reminiscent of traditional markets housed under trees.

The market's canopy serves a dual purpose of providing shade for vendors and collecting rainwater through funnels on its roof, which then flows through hollow 'trunks' and into underground water tanks. These features were designed in consideration of the city's climate, which is characterized by high temperatures and seasonal water shortages.

AFRICAN WATER CITIES

VEGETATION CONTROL

The National Department of Water and Sanitation Cape Town, South Africa, 2018

The natural functioning of healthy watersheds involves the storage, filtration and transportation of rainfall to rivers and lakes. However, in the Greater Cape Town Region, invasive plant species such as acacia, pine and eucalyptus use significant amounts of water, thus compromising aquifer recharge, leading to a reduced water supply for residents in and around Cape Town.

If the watersheds are restored and invasive plants are removed, it could result in an additional 55.6 billion litres of water per year for Cape Town residents. The three-year drought from 2015-2018 left city dams dry, forcing strict rationing. Supported by private sector and community partnerships replicable strategies and toolboxes can aid regions facing water insecurity across Sub-Saharan Africa.

STUDENT ADAPTATION & MITIGATION PROJECTS

Catalysing Aquatic architecture, Lagos, Nigeria

Circles of Hope, Lagos, Nigeria

By Eric Bethany & Masoud Abedi Moghadam

by Masoud Abedimoghadam

Safe-Living , Sedhiou, Senegal

Hydropolis - Silt Lake City, The Nile, Egypt

By Jodel Bismarc Mekemta & Sidoine Constant Takam Kenmogne

By Margaux Ash

WATER CITIES PROJECT ATLAS   255

STUDENT ADAPTATION & MITIGATION PROJECTS

Urban Watering Hole, Zanzibar, Tanzania

Revolving Market Bridge, Lagos, Nigeria

By Kate Kerbel

By Rina Kang

Floating Tower, Lagos, Nigeria

Bridge, Filter, Shop, the Trench, Dar Es Salaam, Tanzania

By Sida Zhang

By Whitney Lang

Title: Edification (Potentiality Series) | Medium: Photography | Size: 80 × 120cm | Year: 2017 | Artist: Alun Be

African Water Cities by NLÉ / Water Cities

African Water Cities will continue to feel the impact of climate change and extreme weather events, while the ongoing population surge, intra-urban migration patterns and economic incentives draw people to the waterfront. This challenges communities, architects, planners and policymakers to rethink how to build and live with water. Sustainable and equitable practices must be at the forefront of any vision for meaningful change.

African coastlines and waterfronts remain some of the most stimulating environments for the birth of innovative building systems, urban strategies and nature-based solutions for future urbanism. This is revealed in projects across the continent, such as a river transformation in Algiers (p 236) and urban rehabilitation in Ganvie (p 238). In Ganvie, the initiative recognizes a community built on water as a potential model for affordable urban development, while keeping impact on the environment minimal. Rwanda, with the Nyabarongo River catchment Plan in Kigali, is mobilizing youths to partake in terrace farming, which reduces water runoff and employs people in terracing, agriculture, and buffer zone management. The Water Cities Project Atlas highlights a selection of tactics where cities impacted by climate change are the stewards for global environmentally responsible solutions. How can designers and policymakers aid developments of frameworks that recognize local knowledge in considering more equitable models that value and support the efforts of the most vulnerable, who are arguably the most adaptable and innovative people within the city? As Ahunna Eziakonwa noted quite poetically, 'it will take this kind of thought leadership and action to get Africa to rise, not against – but with the tide'.

In order to work towards a climate-resilient urban future, both top-down and bottom-up approaches as well as hard and soft infrastructural thinking must work in unison rather than as separate strategies. Similarly, we need to build both the resilience of the most vulnerable populations and the resilience of the city in which they reside. Some of the most innovative climate adaptation practices are not new phenomena and as Taibat Lawanson highlights 'community-based or 'bottom-up' actions debunk the myth that the urban poor are irresponsible custodians of their communities' and instead can help to rethink the need for everyday best practices to be embedded in urban planning processes. [7]

Much of this urbanization is driven by rural-urban migration, as well as population growth. Sub-Saharan Africa is the only region in the world where the population will continue to increase throughout the twenty-first century.[9] Researchers stress that the large youth population should not be excluded or marginalized within their cities. Rather 'youth agency', defined by the United Nations should be embraced, which is 'the ability of young people to make decisions and drive change in their own lives, in their communities, as well as in their larger spheres of influence.' What role does design play to help young people identify their ambitions and provide opportunities for them to engage with their world and their context so that they can collectively thrive? As John May summarizes, 'young people bring innovation and energy, new ideas, risk taking, and entrepreneurship' and when thoughtfully considered, could be a positive driver of economic and healthy growth.[10] To this point, Dr Cristina D'Alessandro describes an effective way of explaining the city not as defined by physical or implied boundaries, but instead defined by the 'concentration of ideas—giving value to the diversity and innovation that will drive the dynamics of change.'[8]

The growing youth population coupled with the intergenerational knowledge of how to build, protect, and thrive with water can be an environmentally just and powerful pathway forward.

Coupling the local knowledge and ecologically intelligent solutions catalogued in The Water Cities Project Atlas with the DESIMER datasets and perspectives from DESIMER experts provides starting points of a comprehensive action plan for targeted development initiatives and achieving Sustainable Development Goals (SDGs). There are gaps in all methods of information collection and analysis, but we see the overlapping of typically distinct datasets—for example urban growth, environmental factors, natural resources, agriculture, et cetera, facts that are typically understood in isolation—as a way to highlight factors that may go overlooked or that help to understand more complex urban-rural-environmental relationships. Furthermore, the overlap of this quantitative information with the qualitative findings from the Atlas begins to form synergies between statistical trends and tested sustainable solutions. For example, our research shows that Benin's economic growth is high. Its agricultural exports make up the largest share of merchandise exports of any African country. And as Hellen Njoki Wanjohi-Opil noted, 'for over four centuries, the historical lake villages of Ganvie in the city of Cotonou in Benin, and Nzulezu in Ghana have existed on water, with structures built on stilts.'[11] How might greater investments in advancing the capacity to live with water help in the health and sustainability of these growing water cities? The opportunity for amplifying aquaculture as a major resource amongst other development potentials of Ganvie, for instance, seems obvious.

As Africa works toward the 17 SDGs that align with the African Union's Agenda 2063,[12] which goals can be foregrounded to engage with the communities today and not in some distant future? One way that this can occur—believe climate and environmental activist, Elizabeth Wathutisuch and Ms. Vera Songwe, UN Under-Secretary-General and UNECA Executive Secretary—is through the acknowledgement that it is the young people who will be most impacted by the SDG. Therefore it is through 'serious' youth engagement, opportunity and employment through the science, technology, engineering, and mathematics (STEM) fields that we can begin to activate change. Through youth advocation we can tackle what Adji Bousso Dieng, Founder of 'The Africa I Know' sees as Africa's biggest problem: unemployment, poverty, and lack of education.[13] We would add architecture, design and the built-environment to also fall under the STEM category and acknowledge the need for technology, design and the humanities to become a united front. These efforts, coupled with cross-continental collaborations such as the African Continental Free Trade Area (AfCFTA) initiatives[14] offer entrepreneurial support for youths such as the 'Youth Protocol', where AfCFTA identify business opportunities in agriculture, technology, finance, and the creative industry for young Africans.[15]

A future that embraces and amplifies the youthfulness of African Water Cities and couples this with education, on-the-ground knowledge, local climate-based design tactics and sound socioeconomic policies can forge an equitable pathway forward. Building on the vision of the first 'Makoko Floating School' prototype, how can we foreground innovative building and infrastructural systems to challenge how cities urbanize around water, foregrounding grassroot knowledge that is scalable? Importantly, how can we continue to conceive of systems that are easily deployed and stitch gaps that may exist within existing communities and cities—whether that is health needs, education, housing, or patterns of movement. The African Water Cities project is just the start of a conversation about how to bring the vast and ever changing conditions of the urbanizing water cities together to thoughtfully work on and design sustainable growth that values a range of voices, expertise, and local tactics.

Thinking about the future, African Water Cities is as daunting as it is exciting. The enormous growth of waterfront regions in all aspects will fuel urban dynamics previously unseen at that scale. As Asia went through a burst of rapid urbanization in recent history, and the Americas before that, the question at hand now is how will Africa continue to urbanize within these trends in decades to come. In this context, the road map to African climate adaptation is to industrialize and integrate key processes to facilitate simple, sustainable building and infrastructure solutions for development; to merge the unplanned with the planned, the global with the vernacular, the formal with the informal, engineered with hands-on, and land with water. For architects and planners, this is a tremendous opportunity to propose a radical, yet very rooted alternative: developing a city with people to think differently, build differently and live differently... with and on water in African cities and communities.

Kunlé Adeyemi, Suzanne Lettieri, Berend Strijland

African Water Cities by NLÉ / Water Cities

Acknowledgements

None of this would have been possible without my amazing team at NLÉ, past and present, and my partner Berend Strijland, whose commitment and loyalty keeps us afloat. Thanks to Suzanne Lettieri for the great academic collaborations we've had over the years and to all the brilliant students that have been part of my research studios at Cornell AAP, Columbia GSAPP, Harvard GSD, and Princeton SoA, all the local institutions we collaborated with as well as the innumerable students that have been inspired by our work. The University of Lagos for my foundation and great support for the African Water Cities Center. To my friends and our supporters at NLÉ / Water Cities following us on this exciting journey.

We are grateful to all the experts, academics, architects, and planners that give this publication its depth and vibrance through their writings, insights, and personal stories.

Huge thanks to the Graham Foundation and the Creative Industries Fund NL for their financial support of this publication. We are deeply grateful to our clients, project partners and supporters, particularly our early adopters who believed in us at times when our ideas still seemed like fiction: the Makoko/Iwaya Waterfront Communities youths and leaders, the United Nations and its agencies, particularly the UNDP, for their intrepid and financial backing; to the Heinrich Böll Stiftung for your good cause, to La Biennale di Venezia, Bruges Triennale, Centre Pompidou, Mao Jihong Arts Foundation, MADStudio, ADS Groupe, Het Nieuwe Instituut, and particularly the heads of these organizations and all the individuals within them who have been instrumental in helping bring the African Water Cities vision to reality.

Like the protagonist in the Babylonian flood story, my late father Noah, to whom I'm eternally grateful, may have been destined to plant the seed of service to humanity and the environment in me. I am thankful for the pride and joy from my loving family—my mother, sister, brother, and other siblings. I am truly blessed with my wonderful wife Vanny and our infant son Noah (Jr.), now in line for his own calling.

ACKNOWLEDGEMENTS

Index

Bibliography

INTRODUCTION

Introduction
By Kunlé Adeyemi

[1] World Meteorological Organisation: State of Climate in Africa highlights water stress and hazards (2022)
[2] United Nations Department of Economic and Social Affairs: World Population Prospects (2022)
[3] AfDB: African Economic Outlook (2022)
[4] World Economic Forum: These 11 sinking cities could disappear by 2100 (2019)
[5] Squires, G. (2014). Chapter 4: Urban Water Economics, Pages 33-43 in Booth, C., and Charlesworth, S. (Eds). (2014). Water Resources in the Built Environment: management issues and solutions, First Edition. Wiley & Sons, Ltd.

RISING POPULATION

Inter-urban migration in African Waterfront Cities
By Irit Ittner

[1] C. Nunes Silva (Ed.), Urban planning in Sub-Saharan Africa: Colonial and post-colonial planning cultures (New York: Routledge, 2015).
[2] M. Gidel, M., Fragmentation on the waterfront: Coastal squatting settlements and urban renewal projects in the Caribbean. In: G. Desfor et al. (Eds.), Transforming urban waterfronts. Fixity and flows (New York/ London: Routledge, 2011), 35-54. G. Desfor and J. Laidley, Introduction: Fixity and flow in urban waterfront change, in: G. Desfor et al., Transforming urban waterfronts: Fixity and flows (New York/ London: Routledge, 2011), 1-13.
[3] S. Croese 'Global urban policy making in Africa: A view from Angola through the redevelopment of the Bay of Luanda', International Journal of Urban and Regional Research 42 (2018), 198-209. I. Adjibade, 'Can a future city enhance urban resilience and sustainability? A political ecology analysis of Eko Atlantic city, Nigeria', International Journal of Disaster Risk Reduction 26 (2017), 85-92.
[4] C.H. Wizor and C.A. Emerueh 'Perceived impact of urban waterfront dwellers' forced eviction on housing, security and social support system in Njemanze and Otodo-Gbame informal settlements, Nigeria', Asian Research Journal of Arts & Social Sciences 10 (2020), 43-56. Eguavoen 'Reclamation and expulsion: Frontiers of city expansion and the loss of public and communal space at Abidjan's lagoonal waterfronts', Urban Forum 33 (2022), 367–92.
[5] K. Fakoya et al., Understanding vulnerabilities of urban waterfront communities to rapid development: The case of Lagos Lagoon, Nigeria, in: S. Jenthof et al. (Eds.) Blue Justice. Small-scale fisheries in a sustainable ocean economy (Cham: Springer, 2022), 451-467.
[6] F. Frick-Trzebitzky, F. et al. 'Institutional bricolage and the production of vulnerability to floods in an urbanizing delta in Accra', International Journal of Disaster Risk Reduction 26 (2017), 57-68. P. Stacey, State of slum: Precarity and informal governance at the margins of Accra (ZED, 2019). P.G. Innes 'Official Risks and Everyday Disasters: the Interplay of Riskscapes in Two Unplanned Settlements in Monrovia', Urban Forum (2021) https://doi.org/10.1007/s12132-022-09465-9
[7] I. Eguavoen et al. 'Dernier refuge ou presqu'île d'opportunités? Démographie et conditions de vie à Adjahui-Coubé, un habitat spontané à Abidjan', ZEF Working Paper 187 (2020), Bonn.
[8] Ibid.
[9] D. Simon (Ed.), Re-thinking sustainable cities: Accessible, green and fair (Bristol: Policy Press, 2016).
[10] M. Davidson, Urban Geography: Waterfront development, in: N. Thrift and R. Kitchen (Eds.), International Encyclopedia of Human Geography (Oxford: Elsevier, 2009), 215-221.
[11] I. Eguavoen 'Reclamation and expulsion: Frontiers of city expansion and the loss of public and communal space at Abidjan's lagoonal waterfronts', Urban Forum 33 (2022), 367–92.

Africa's Rising Urban and Water Population
By John F. May

[1] United Nations (2022a). World Population Prospects 2022. New York, NY: United Nations, Department of Economic and Social Affairs, Population Division.
[2] United Nations (2022b). Young People's Potential, the Key to Africa's Sustainable Development. New York, NY: Office for the High Representative for the Least Developed Countries, Landlocked Developing Countries and Small Islands Developing States; see https://www.un.org/ohrlls/news/young-people%E2%80%99s-potential-key-africa%E2%80%99s-sustainable-development, accessed on January 17, 2023.
[3] Population Reference Bureau (2022). World Population Data Sheet 2022. Washington, DC: Population Reference Bureau.
[4] United Nations (2019). World urbanization Urbanization Prospects: The 2018 Revision. New York, NY: United Nations, Department of Economic and Social Affairs, Population Division.
[5] Vučković, M. and A. M. Adams (2022). "Population and Health Policies in Urban Areas". Chapter 18 (Pp. 397-429) in May, J. F. and J. A. Goldstone (Eds), International Handbook of Population Policies, Cham, CH: Springer.
[6] Fengler, W. (2010). Can rapid population growth be good for economic development? Washington, DC: World Bank Group. Retrieved from https://blogs.worldbank.org/africacan/can-rapid-population-growth-be-good-for-economic-development.
[7] McGreevey, W., A. Acharya, J. S. Hammer, and L. MacKellar (2008). "Propinquity Matters: How Better Health, urbanization Urbanization, and Income Grew Together, 1870-2008". The Georgetown Journal of Poverty Law & Policy XV(3): 605-633.
[8] Groth, H. and J. F. May (2017). Africa's Population: In Search of a Demographic Dividend. Cham, CH: Springer.

RISING WATER

Water, the Cradle and Coffin of Civilization
By Steven Mithen

[1] Mithen, S.J. 2012. Thirst: Water and Power in the Ancient World. London: Weidenfeld & Nicholson
[2] Mithen, S.J. & Black, E. (eds) 2011. Water, Life and Civilisation: Climate, Environment and Society in the Jordan Valley. Cambridge: Cambridge University Press.
[3] He, C., Liu, Z., Wu, J. et al. 2021. Future global urban water scarcity and potential solutions. Nature Communications 12, 4667.
[4] Fujii, S. 2010. A comprehensive review of Neolithic water catchment facilities in the Jafr Basin, southern Jordan: A preliminary report of the Jafr Basin Prehistoric Project (Phase 3), 2009. Annual of the Department of Antiquities of Jordan 54, 371-386.
[5] Galili, E. & Nir, Y. 1993. The submerged Pre-Pottery Neolithic water well of Atlit-Yam, northern Israel and its palaeoenvironmental implications. The Holocene 3, 265-70.
[6] Garfinkel, Y., vered, A. & Bar-Yosef, O. 2006. The domestication of water: the late Neolithic well at Sha'ar Hagolan, Jordan valley, Israel. Antiquity 80, 686-96.
[7] Whitehead, P.G. Smith, S.J., Wade, A., Mithen, S.J., Finlayson, B, & Sellwood, B. 2008. Modelling of hydrology and potential population levels at Bronze Age Jawa northern Jordan: a Monte Carlo approach to cope with uncertainty. Journal of Archaeological Science 35, 517-29.
[8] Postgate, N. J.N. 1992. Early Mesopotamia: Society and Economy at the Dawn of History. London: Routledge.
[9] Jacobsen, T. & Adams, R.A. 1958. Salt and silt in Ancient Mesopotamian agriculture. Science 3334, 1251-8.
[10] Tamburrino, A. 2010. Water technology in Ancient Mesopotamia. In Ancient Water Technologies (ed. L. mays), pp. 29-51. Dordrecht; Springer.
[11] Oleson, J. 2007. Nabataean water supply, irrigation and agriculture: an overview. In The World of the Nabataeans (ed. K.D. Politis), pp. 217-49. Stuttgart: Franz Steiner Verlag.
[12] Bedal, L.-A., & Schryver, J.G. 2007. Nabataean landscape and power: evidence from the Petra garden and pool complex. In Crossing Jordan: North America Contributions to the Archaeology of Jordan. (eds. T.E. Levy, P.M. Daviau & R.W. Youker), pp. 375-83. London: Equinox Publishing.

Navigating The Impacts Of Climate Change
By Hellen Njoki Wanjohi-Opil

[1] OECD &SWAC. (2020). Africa's urbanization Dynamics 2020: Africapolis, Mapping a New Urban Geography, West African Studies, OECD Publishing, Paris, https://doi.org/10.1787/b6bccb81-en. (p.72 & 73).
[2] Novotny, Vladimir & Brown, Paul. (2007). Cities of the Future: Towards Integrated Sustainable Water and Landscape Management. IWA Publishing, London, UK, 352 pp.
[3] Freund, Bill. (2007). The African City: A History. Cambridge University Press, Cambridge, UK, 214 pp. (p.3)
[4] OECD & SWAC (2020), Africa's urbanization Dynamics 2020: Africapolis, Mapping a New Urban Geography, West African Studies, OECD Publishing, Paris, https://doi.org/10.1787/b6bccb81-en. (p.120).
[5] IPCC. (2022). Climate Change 2022: Impacts, Adaptation, and Vulnerability. Contribution of Working Group II to the Sixth Assessment Report of the Intergovernmental Panel on Climate Change [H.-O. Pörtner, D.C. Roberts, M. Tignor, E.S. Poloczanska, K. Mintenbeck, A. Alegría, M. Craig, S. Langsdorf, S. Löschke, V. Möller, A. Okem, B. Rama (eds.)]. Cambridge University Press, Cambridge, UK and New York, NY, USA, 3056 pp., doi:10.1017/9781009325844.
[6] Lagos floods: Africa's most populous city could be unlivable in a few decades, experts warn | CNN.
[7] Beira: A city's fight against climate change – DW – 10/23/2021.
[8] The Nile river led to Khartoum's growth, but now threatens the city (theconversation.com).
[9] Feisal, Zeinab & Haron, Ahmed. (2020). Coastal Cities Resilience for Climate Change Case Study: Egyptian North Coast Cities. 10.13140/RG.2.2.31192.65289.
[10 Photos show Senegal neighborhood disappearing as sea levels rise - The Washington Post.
[11] Shepherd A., Mitchell T., Lewisk, K., Lenhardt, A., Jones, L., Scott, L. & Muir-Wood R. (2013). The Geography of Poverty, Disasters and Climate Extremes in 2030. Overseas Development Institute, London, 72pp.
[12] Ganvie – The African Village Built Entirely On Stilts - TalkAfricana.
[13] Africa Center for Strategic Studies, "Rising Sea Levels and Africa's Booming Coastal Cities", Infographic, November 8th 2022.
[14] Patrick D. Nunn, Carola Klöck, Virginie Duvat. Seawalls as Maladaptations along Island Coasts. Ocean & Coastal Management, Volume 205, 2021, 105554, https://doi.org/10.1016/j.ocecoaman.2021.105554.

Demographic Pressures of Water Supply in Cities
By Winnie Mitullah

[1][2] UNESCO. United Nations World Water Development Report 2021 – Valuing Water. Geneva: UN Water (Paris, UNESCO, 2021)
[3] Gulyani, S., Talukdar, D., and Kariuki, M.R. Water for the Urban Poor: Water Markets, Household Demand, and Service Preferences in Kenya. World Bank, Washington DC, Water Supply and Sanitation Sector Board, DP No. 5, 2005.
[4] WHO/UNICEF. Joint Monitoring Programme for Water Supply and Sanitation. Technical Task Force Meeting on Monitoring Progress in Water Supply and Sanitation – Challenges in Water Urban Settings, 6 – 9 June, 2011, Nanyuki, Kenya. Geneva: WHO
[5] OECD. 2021. Water Governance in African Cities. OECD Studies on Water. OECD Publishing, Paris. https://doi/10.1787/19effb77-en accessed on 7 November 2022
[6] Manna, K.M. 2019. Nature-Based Technologies for Africa's Waste Water Challenges. https://news.grida.no/naturebased-technology-forAfrica's-Wastewater-challenges accessed on 22 October, 2022
[7] Hajjar, B. 2020. The Children's Continent: Keeping with Africa's Growth. World Economic Forum. https://www.weforum.org/agenda/2020/01/the-children-s-continent/ accessed on 18 October, 2022
[8] Beard, V.A. and Mitlin, D. 2021. Water access in Global South Cities: The Challenge of intermittency and affordability. World Development, 147 (2021), (105625)

7 DESIMER FACTORS OF URBAN SUSTAINABLE DEVELOPMENT

Demographics
By Christopher Changwe Nshimbi

[1] Nshimbi, C. C., & Fioramonti, L. (2013). A Region Without Borders? Policy Frameworks for Regional Labour Migration Towards South Africa. African Centre for Migration & Society, University of the Witwatersrand.
[2] United Nations Department of Economic and Social Affairs Population Division. (2022). World Population Prospects 2022: Summary of Results. https://www.un.org/development/desa/pd/sites/www.un.org.development.desa.pd/files/wpp2022_summary_of_results.pdf
[3] World Health Organization. Regional Office for Africa. (2022). Tracking universal health coverage in the WHO African Region, 2022. http://apps.who.int/iris/bitstream/handle/10665/361229/9789290234760-eng.pdf?sequence=3
[4] UN Habitat. (2021). Regional Office for Africa - Annual Report. www.unhabitat.org
[5] Farrell, K. (2017). The Rapid Urban Growth Triad: A New Conceptual Framework for Examining the Urban Transition in Developing Countries. Sustainability, 9(8), 1407. https://doi.org/10.3390/su9081407
[6] UN Habitat. (2016). Habitat III Regional Report Africa-Transformational Housing and Sustainable Urban Development in Africa. https://habitat3.org/wp-content/uploads/Habitat-III-Regional-Report-Africa.pdf

[7] Mercandalli, S., & Nshimbi, C. C. (2016). Migration Dynamics: Contrasted Patterns, Diversity and Potential. In D. Pesche, B. Losch, & J. Imbernon (Eds.), A New Emerging Rural World. An Overview of Rural Change in Africa. Atlas for the NEPAD Rural Futures Programme (p. 76). Cirad. https://www.cirad.fr/en/publications-resources/publishing/studies-and-documents/atlas-a-new-emerging-rural-world-in-africa-2nd-edition

Economics
By Joy Antonia Kategekwa

[1] UNDP Human Development Report. Uncertain times, Unsettled lives: Shaping our future in a transforming world. Online available: https://hdr.undp.org/content/human-development-report-2021-22.
[2] World Bank, GDP Growth (annual), sub Saharan Africa. Online available: https://data.worldbank.org/indicator/NY.GDP.MKTP.KD.ZG?locations=ZG.
[3] For economic growth forecasts for Southern Africa see: IMF, "Living on the edge": Online available: https://www.imf.org/en/Publications/REO/SSA/Issues/2022/10/14/regional-economic-outlook-for-sub-saharan-africa-october-2022.
[4] Inflation, Consumer Prices (annual), sub – saran Africa. Online available: https://data.worldbank.org/indicator/FP.CPI.TOTL.ZG?end=2021&locations=ZG-GH&start=1965&view=chart.
[5] The World Bank in Ghana. Overview. Online available: https://www.worldbank.org/en/country/ghana/overview.
[6] AfDB, "Africa's economic growth to outpace global forecast in 2023-2024 – African Development Bank biannual report"
[7] See The largest shipping companies – Top 10. Ship hub. Online available: https://www.shiphub.co/the-largest-shipping-companies/.
[8] World Bank, "Countries Could Cut Emissions by 70% by 2050 and Boost Resilience with Annual Investments of 1.4% of GDP". Online available: https://www.worldbank.org/en/news/press-release/2022/11/03/countries-could-cut-emissions-by-70-by-2050-and-boost-resilience-with-annual-investments-of-1-4-of-gdp. Accessed 8 February 2023.
[9] United Nations Foundation " The Sustainable Development Goals in 2019: People, Planet, Prosperity in Focus". Online available: https://unfoundation.org/blog/post/the-sustainable-development-goals-in-2019-people-planet-prosperity-in-focus/.
[10] World Meteorological Organization (WMO), "State of Climate in Africa highlights water stress and hazards". Online available: https://public.wmo.int/en/media/press-release/state-of-climate-africa-highlights-water-stress-and-hazards#:~:text=%E2%80%9CAfrica's%20climate%20has%20warmed%20more,salinity%20in%20low%2Dlying%20cities..
[11] Oguntola, Tunde, "2022 Flood: 603 Dead, 1.3m Displaced Across Nigeria – Federal Govt". Online available: https://en.wikipedia.org/wiki/2022_Nigeria_floods#cite_note-2.
[12] Wikipedia, "Africa Floods 2022: Online available: https://en.wikipedia.org/wiki/2022_Africa_floods#:~:text=Floods%20in%20April%20killed%2020,Floods%20there%20killed%20169%20people.
[13] Africa Climate Mobility Report, "African shifts – climate disruption in a continent on the move". Online available: https://africa.climatemobility.org/overview#african-shifts.
[14] Ibid.
[15] Council for Foreign Relations, "Climate Change and Conflict in the Sahel". Online available: https://www.cfr.org/report/climate-change-and-conflict-sahel#:~:text=Climate%20change%20predictions%20indicate%20that,other%20parts%20of%20the%20world.
[16] See PIDA. https://au.int/en/ie/pida.

Socio-Politics
By Taibat Lawwanson

Infrastructure
By Denis W. Aheto & Peter Kristensen

[1] https://documents.worldbank.org/curated/en/822421552504665834/pdf/135269-Madji-49741-WACA-COED-Report-Web-March-13.pdf
[2] https://www.worldbank.org/en/region/afr/publication/west-africas-coast-losing-over-38-billion-a-year-to-erosion-flooding-and-pollution
[3] Climate Change 2014. Niang et al., 2014
[4] https://www.penaf.org/
[5] https://www.ecoports.com/
[6] https://green-marine.org/
[7] https://acecor.ucc.edu.gh/
[8] https://acecor.ucc.edu.gh/

Morphology
By Christina D'Alessandro

[1] C. D'Alessandro-Scarpari, 'Le metropoli africane, tracce di storia per oltrepassare la crisi. Appunti per una gestione alternativa dei territori urbani', in: V. Bini and Vitale M. Ney (eds.), Incontri a margine. Culture urbane nell'Africa contemporanea (Milano: Franco Angeli, 2012), 15-24.
[2] M. Dumont and C. D'Alessandro-Scarpari C., La clé des villes (Paris: Le Cavalier Bleu Editions, 2007).
[3] D'Alessandro C., (2017), 'Resource Geographies in Urban Spaces. Insights from Developing Countries in the Post-2015 Era', in: Besada H., Polonenko L., and Agarwal M. (eds), Did the MDGs work? Meeting Future Challenges with Past Lessons (Bristol: Policy Press, 2017), 99-117.
[4] S.E. Lantos, S.V. Lall and Nancy Lozano-Gracias, The Morphology of African Cities (Washington DC: World Bank Group, December 2016).
[5] G. Myers, African Cities. Alternative Visions of Urban Theory and Practice (London-New York: Zed Books, 2011).
[6] AM. Simone & A. Abouhani (eds.), Urban Africa. Changing Contours of Survival in the City (Dakar: CODESRIA, 2005).
[7] C. D'Alessandro, K.T. Hanson and Kararach G., 'Peri-urban agriculture in Southern Africa: miracle or mirage?', African Geographical Review, October 4, (2016), 1-24.
[8] V. Bini V. and C. D'Alessandro (2017), 'New Spaces of Inequalities: Middle- and Upper-Class Real Estate Projects in West Africa', Territorio, 81 (Milano: Franco Angeli, 2017), 31-33.
[9] S. Dasgupta, B. Laplante, C. Meisner, D. Wheeler, & J. Yan, 'The Impact of Sea Level Rise on Developing Countries. A Comparative Analysis', World Bank Policy Research Working Paper, 4136, 2007.
[10] A.L. Lambert and C. D'Alessandro, 'Sea Level Rise and National Security Challenge of Sustainable Urban Adaptation in Doha and Other Arab Coastal Cities', in: Cochrane L. and Al-Hababi R. (eds.), Sustainable Qatar. Social, Political and Environmental Perspectives (London: Routledge, 2023), 147-165.
[11] M.E. ToK, C. D'Alessandro, A. Akinsemolu and B. Khaled B., 'Zero Waste Cities in the Developing World: A Comparative Study", in: Ali S.N. and Jumat Z.H. (eds.), Islamic Finance and Circular Economy. Connecting Impact and Value Creation (Singapore, Springer: 2021), 241-259.
[12] African Development Bank, Development Perspectives on Special Agro-industrial Processing Zones in Africa: Lessons from Experiences, (Abidjan: African Development Bank, 2021).
[13] C. D'Alessandro and F. Léautier, Cities and Spaces of Leadership: A Geographical Perspective (London: Palgrave Macmillan, 2016).

Environment
By Vincent N. Ojeh

[1] Mbaye, A.A. (2020). Confronting the challenges of climate change on Africa's coastal areas. Brookings-Africa in focus. Editor's note, Thursday, January 16, 2020, pp 1-5
[2] Kennedy-Walker, R., Amezaga, J. M. & Paterson, C.A. (2015). The impact of community social dynamics on achieving improved sanitation access for the urban poor: The case of Lusaka, Zambia. Habitat International 50 (4):326-334. DOI: 10.1016/j.habitatint.2015.09.004
[3] Adelekan, I.O. (2010). Vulnerability of poor urban coastal communities to flooding in Lagos, Nigeria. Environment & Urbanization. Vol 22(2): 433–450. DOI: 10.1177/0956247810380141
[4] Eisenschmidt, A & Adeyemi. K. (2012). African Water Cities. Architectural Design 82(5), DOI: 10.1002/ad.1468
[5] Vitousek, S., P. L. Barnard, & P. Limber (2017). Can beaches survive climate change?, J. Geophys. Res. Earth Surf., 122, 1060–1067, doi:10.1002/2017JF004308.
[6] Neumann, B., Vafeidis, A. T., Zimmermann, J., & Nicholls, R. J. (2015). Future Coastal Population Growth and Exposure to Sea-Level Rise and Coastal Flooding - A Global Assessment. PLOS ONE, 10(3), e0118571. https://doi.org/10.1371/journal.pone.0118571
[8] Haider, H. (2019). Climate change in Nigeria: impacts and responses. K4D Helpdesk Report,1–38. Retrievedfrom:http://www.rockfound.org/initiatives/climate/climate_change.shtml%0Awww.id.org/HS/publications.html.%0AHOW%0Ahttps://assets.publishing.service.gov.uk/media/5dcd7a1aed915d0719bf4542/675_Climate_Change_in_Nigeria.pdf
[9] Elias, P., & Omojola, A. (2015). Case study: The challenges of climate change for Lagos, Nigeria. Current Opinion in Environmental Sustainability, 13, 74-78. https://doi.org/10.1016/j.cosust.2015.02.008
[10] Cobbinah, P.B. & Addaney, M. (2018). The Geography of Climate Change Adaptation in Urban Africa. DOI: 10.1007/978-3-030-04873-0_19
[11] Buhari, M., A. O. Akintuyi, A. S. Barau, G Edaogbogun, O.A. Muraina & D. O. Ayodele-Olajire (2021). Adaptation to Climate Change in Lagos: Managing Flood Risk Through Sustainable Waste Management- Technical Report. Inter Campus Alliance on sustainable Cities (ICASC) Innovation Team Project report February 2021, pp 1-26
[12] Powell, J., R.M Chertow & Daniel C.E. (2018). Where is global waste management heading? An analysis of solid waste sector commitments from nationally-determined contributions. Waste Management 80:137-143. DOI: 10.1016/j.wasman.2018.09.008
[13] Koop, S.H.A., Koetsier, L., Doornhof, A. O. Reinstra, C. J. Van Leeuwen, S. Brouwer, C. Dieperink & P. P. J. Driessen. (2017) Assessing the Governance Capacity of Cities to Address Challenges of Water, Waste, and Climate Change. Water Resour Manage 31, 3427–3443 (2017). https://doi.org/10.1007/s11269-017-1677-7
[14] Lagos Resilience Strategy (2020). Lagos Resilience Strategy. Retrieved from http://www.lagosresilience.net/Downloads/Lagos_Resilience_Strategy.pdf

Resources
By Ngozi Finette Unuigbe and Omon Aigbbokhaevbo

[1] Charles A Ray, 'The Impact of Climate Change on Africa's Economy' (Foreign Policy Research Institute, October 29, 2021) < https://www.fpri.org/article/2021/10/the-impact-of-climate-change-on-africas-economies/ > accessed 9 January 2023
[2] Dan Shepherd, Global Warming; Severe Consequences for Africa' (2021 <https://www.un.org/africarenewal/magazine/december-2018-march-2019/global-warming-severe-> accessed 9 January 2023
[3] Satterthwaite, D., S. Huq, H. Reid, M. Pelling, and P. R. Lankao. 2007. 'Adapting to Climate Change in Urban Areas: The Possibilities and Constraints in Low-and Middle-Income Nations.' (2019) <http://pubs.iied.org/pdfs/10549IIED.pdf > accessed 9 January, 2023.
[4] World Economic Forum, 'African Cities will double in Population by 2050. Here are 4 ways to make sure they thrive' (2018)< https://www.weforum.org/agenda/2018/06/Africa-urbanization urbanization-cities-double- population-2050-4%20 ways-thrive/ > accessed 9 January, 2023
[5] Lake Chad Basin hereinafter abbreviated as LCB is located in Northern Central Africa and borders four countries- Chad, Nigeria, Niger and Cameroon.
[6] Abihjit. Mohanty, Kieran Robson, Samuel Njueping, Swayam Sampurna Nanda, (DownToEarth 23 February 2021) 'Climate Change, Conflict: What is fuelling the Lake Chad crisis?'<https://www.google.com/amp/s/www.downtoearth.org.in/blog/climate%2520change/amp/climate-change-conflict-what-is-fuelling-the-lake-chad-crisis-75639 > accessed 8 Jan 2023
[7] Zeiba, F. W., Yenogh, G. T., and Tom, A. (2017), 'Seasonal Migration and Settlement around Lake Chad: Strategies for Control of Resources in an Increasingly Drying Lake'. Resources (2017), 6, 41. Doi: 103390/resources603004 accessed 8 Jan 2023.
[8] A. B Alhassan, A.M Chiroma, A.M Kundiri, B. Babawe, I.J Tekwa, 'Decline in Agricultural Activity Around Lake Chad: Any Prospects for Restoration: A Review' (2021) Arid Zone Journal of Engineering, Technology and Environment, Vol 17(2) 221-230
[9] A. A. Amali, M. S. Bala, and F. A. Adeniji, 'Dying Lake Chad: 'Adaptive strategies to climate change and water scarcity of the lake chad basin,' in Proceedings of the Water Management in a Changing World: Role of Irrigation for Sustainable Food Production Chiang-Mai, Thailand, November 2016.
[10] Antonio Sampiano, 'Conflict Economies and Urban Systems in the Lake Chad Region' (2022) <shorturl.at/dmCO6 > accessed 8 January 2023.
[11] Ellen Wolfhurst, ' World's Urban Growth will surge more in India, China and Nigeria- UN' (2018, Reuters) < https://www.reuters.com/article/us-global-population-cities-idUSKCN1IH2RO.> accessed 26 January 2023
[12] Supra 10
[13] Brodie Ramin, 'Slums, Climate Change and Human Health in Sub-Saharan Africa, <https://www.ncbi.nlm.nih.gov/pmc/articles/PMC2789375/ > accessed 9 Jan 2023.
[14] Bjorn Arnsten, 'Forced Migrants navigating the Boko Haram Crisis-Continuities and Discontinues' < https://scienceetbiencommun.pressbooks.pub/nord-cameroun/chapter/125/ > accessed 9 Jan 2023
[15] United Nations, 'Climate Change Focus: Lake Chad trees keep deadly drought at bay' (2018) <https://news.un.org/en/story/2018/11/1026651 >accessed 9 January 2023.

16 Mark Schrivjer, Josue Bangua, 'COP 27: The African COP and the risk of a global U-turn to the Paris Agreement' (World Bank, November 17, 2022)< https://blogs.worldbank.org/africacan/cop27-african- cop-and-risk-global-u-turn-paris-agreement > accessed 9 Jan 2023

17 COPs referring to Conference of Parties are United Nations Climate Summits which are held every year for governments across the world to agree steps to limit global temperature levels. See here, <https://www.google.com/amp/s/ www.bbc.com/news/science-environment-63316362.amp > accessed 9 January 2023.

18 The commission was established in 1964 by the four countries bordering the Lake Chad Region. See here <https://cblt.org/ > accessed 9 January 2023

19 UNESCO, 'Promoting Peace in the Lake Chad Basin through the successful management of its resources' (2017) < https://www. unesco.org/en/articles/promoting-peace-lake-chad-basin-through-sustainable-management-its-resources > accessed 25 Jan 2023.

20 LCBC, 'Regional Project for the Conservation and Sustainable Development of Lake Chad' (2021) <https://cblt.org/regional-project-for-the-conservation-and-sustainable-development-of-lake-chad/> accessed 25 January 2023

21 Water Charter of the Lake Chad Basin 2011

22 United Nations, Convention on the Protection and Use of Transboundary Water Resources and International Lakes (1992)

23 World Economic Forum, 'Afforestation can help to tackle Climate Change' (2021) <shorturl.at/uxDJO> accessed 26 January 2023.

TOP 20 AFRICAN WATER CITIES

Methodology

[1] OpenAI. "OpenAI." OpenAI, openai.com. (accessed March 2023).

DESIMER Index
Demographics

[1] United Nations.Population Division (2022) .Births (thousands). [online] ourworldindata.org Available at: https://population.un.org/wpp/Download/Standard/MostUsed/ Retrieved from:https://ourworldindata.org/grapher/crude-birth-rate?tab=chart

[2] UN Food and Agriculture Organization (FAO)(2020). Population density in Africa. [online] Available at: https://www.theglobaleconomy.com/rankings/population_density/Africa/

[3] The World Bank (2021). Urban population growth (annual %) - Sub-Saharan Africa | Data. [online] Available at: https://data.worldbank.org/indicator/SP.URB.GROW?locations=ZG&name_desc=false.

[4] World Population Review. (n.d.). Africa Cities by Population 2023. [online] Available at: https://worldpopulationreview.com/continents/africa/cities.

Economics

[1] The World Bank (2021). GDP per capita, PPP by country, around the world [online] TheGlobalEconomy.com. Available at: https://www.theglobaleconomy.com/rankings/GDP_per_capita_PPP/.

[2] The World Bank (2021). Economic growth by country, around the world. [online] TheGlobalEconomy.com Available at: https://www.theglobaleconomy.com/rankings/Economic_growth/.

[3] The World Bank (2020). Inflation, GDP deflator (annual %) | Data. [online] Available at: https://data.worldbank.org/indicator/NY.GDP.DEFL.KD.ZG?end=2020&start=2005

[4] International Monetary Fund (2020). Foreign Direct Investment, net (BoP, currency US$). [online] databank. worldbank.org Available at: https://databank.worldbank.org/reports.aspx?source=2&series=BN.KLT.DINV.CD&country

Socio-politics

[1] Transparency International (2021). 2021 Corruptions Perceptions Index. [online] Available at: https://www.transparency.org/en/cpi/2021.

[2] IDMC (2021). 2021 Global Report on Internal Displacement. [online] Available at: https://www.internal-displacement.org/global-report/grid2021/.

[3] World Economic Forum (n.d.). Global Gender Gap Report 2022 - Insight Report July 2022. [online] Available at: https://www3.weforum.org/docs/WEF_GGGR_2022.pdf.

[4] Thomas Hale, Noam Angrist, Rafael Goldszmidt, Beatriz Kira, Anna Petherick, Toby Phillips, Samuel Webster, Emily Cameron-Blake, Laura Hallas, Saptarshi Majumdar, and Helen Tatlow. (2021). "A global panel database of pandemic policies (Oxford COVID-19 Government Response Tracker)." Nature Human Behaviour. https://doi.org/10.1038/s41562-021-01079-8 [online] Available at: https://www.bsg.ox.ac.uk/research/research-projects/oxford-covid-19-government-response-tracker Retrieved from: https://ourworldindata.org/grapher/covid-containment-and-health-index

Infrastructure

[1] UNCTAD (2020). Container port traffic (TEU: 20 foot equivalent units) | Data.data.worldbank.org [online] Available at: https://data.worldbank.org/indicator/IS.SHP.GOOD.TU

[2] The World Bank and Turku School of Economics (2018). Logistics performance index: Quality of trade and transport-related infrastructure (1=low to 5=high) - Cabo Verde | Data. [online] Available at: https://data.worldbank.org/indicator/LP.LPI.INFR.XQ?locations=CV&most_recent_year_desc=true&view=map [Accessed 3 Apr. 2023].

[3] International Telecommunication Union (ITU) World Telecommunication/ICT Indicators Database (2021). Individuals using the Internet (% of population) | Data. [online] data.worldbank.org Available at: https://data.worldbank.org/indicator/IT.NET.USER.ZS?view=map&year=2020/

[4] CAIT Climate Data Explorer via Climate Watch (2020). Per capita CO2 emissions from transport. [online] www.climatewatchdata.org Available at: https://www.climatewatchdata.org/data-explorer/historical-emissions Retrieved from:https://ourworldindata.org/grapher/per-capita-co2-transport

Morphology

[1] United Nations Human Settlements Programme (UN-HABITAT) (2020). Population living in slums (% of urban population). [online] /databank.worldbank.org Available at: https://databank.worldbank.org/reports.aspx?source=2&series=EN.POP.SLUM.UR.ZS&country=.

[2] World Development Indicators - World Bank (2022). Share of people living in urban areas. Datacatalog.worldbank.org [online] Available at: datacatalog.worldbank.orghttps://datacatalog.worldbank.org/search/dataset/0037712/World-Development-Indicators. Retrieved from: https://ourworldindata.org/grapher/share-of-population-urban

[3] The World Bank (2020). Access to electricity (% of population) | Data. [online] data.worldbank.org. https://data.worldbank.org/indicator/EG.ELC.ACCS.ZS?view=map.

[4] Google Earth. (2023). Google Earth. [online] Available at: https://earth.google.com [Accessed 3 Apr. 2023].

Environment

[1] UN Food and Agriculture Organization (FAO) (2019). Average precipitation in depth (mm per year) - Sub-Saharan Africa. [online] data.worldbank.org Available at: https://data.worldbank.org/indicator/AG.LND.PRCP.MM?locations=ZG.

[2][4] Internal Displacement Monitoring Centre. (2021). Global Internal Displacement Database. [online] Available at: https://www.internal-displacement.org/database/displacement-data.

[3] Statista. (n.d.). Africa: flood risk 2022. [online] Available at: https://www.statista.com/statistics/1313372/physical-exposure-to-floods-by-country-africa/ [Accessed 3 Apr. 2023].

Resources

[1] The World Bank (n.d.). Natural resources income by country, around the world. [online] TheGlobalEconomy.com. Available at: https://www.theglobaleconomy.com/rankings/Natural_resources_income/

[2] UN Food and Agriculture Organization (FAO). Forest Resources Assessment 2020. (2019). Share of land covered by forest. [online] Available at: https://fra-data.fao.org/ retrieved from https://ourworldindata.org/grapher/forest-area-as-share-of-land-area [3UN Food and Agriculture Organization (FAO) (2019). 6.4.2 Water stress | Sustainable Development Goals. [online] www.fao.org. Available at: https://www.fao.org/sustainable-development-goals/indicators/642/en/#:~:text=The%20level%20of%20water%20stress [Accessed 3 Apr. 2023].

[4] The World Bank (2021). Agricultural raw materials exports (% of merchandise exports) | Data. [online] data.worldbank.org. Available at: https://data.worldbank.org/indicator/TX.VAL.AGRI.ZS.UN.

Data Sources

[1] www.xpatulator.com. (n.d.). International Cost of Living Expat Calculator. [online] Available at: https://www.xpatulator.com/.

[2] www.numbeo.com. (n.d.). Africa: Price Rankings by Country of Water (1.5 liter bottle) (Markets). [online] Available at: https://www.numbeo.com/cost-of-living/country_price_rankings?displayCurrency=USD&itemId=13&region=002 [Accessed 3 Apr. 2023].

WATER CITIES ATLAS

Adaptation & Mitigation
By Berend Strijland

[1] World Population Prospects 2022, United Nations Publication, 2022
[2] Intergovernmental Panel on Climate Change, IPCC. 2022
[3] Urban Flood risk management in Africa, Brian Lucas 2020.
[4] The Cuvelai Basin, John Mendelsohn and Beat Webere, 2011
[5] The Ondjiva Paradox, D Magazine, by J. Makhoul 2013
[6] Mapping 21st Century Global Coastal Land Reclamation, Dhritiraj Sengupta, Young Rae Choi, Bo Tian et al., 2023
[8] Reclamation and Expulsion. Frontiers of City Expansion and the Loss of Public and Communal Spaces at Abidjan's Lagoonal Waterfronts, I. Eguavoen 2022
[9] Urbanization and Floods in Sub-Saharan Africa: Spatiotemporal Study and Analysis of Vulnerability Factors. Fenosoa Nantenaina Ramiaramanana and Jacques Teller, 2021.

Water Cities Project Atlas

[1] "Kenya: Mangrove Restoration at Gazi Bay." Society for Ecological Restoration https://www.ser-rrc.org/project/kenya-mangrove-restoration-at-gazi-bay/.
https://www.unhcr.org/news/briefing/2022/10/635251694/devastation-south-sudan-following-fourth-year-historic-floods.html https://www.researchgate.net/publication/282533081_Departure_from_Indigenous_Land_Use_System_and_the_Consequential_Impacts_A_Case_of_Cuvelai_Basin_North-Central_Namibia https://www.dutchwatersector.com/news/massive-4-km-levee-along-niger-river-provides-flood-protection-for-city-of-mopti-mali

OUTLOOK
Kunlé Adeyemi, Suzanne Lettieri, Berend Strijland

[1] "Navigating The Impacts Of Climate Change," Hellen Njoki Wanjohi-Opil.
[2] "Intra-urban Migration in African Waterfront Cities," Irit Ittner.
[3] "Demographic Pressures of Water Supply in Cities," Winnie V. Mitullah.
[4] "Growing With the Tide: African Water Cities in the Climate Emergency," Dr Joy Antonia Kategekwa.
[5] "Africa. Continent on the move, within itself," Christopher Changwe Nshimbi.
[6] "Navigating The Impacts Of Climate Change," Hellen Njoki Wanjohi-Opil.
[7] "Socio-Political factors of development: a view from Lagos," Taibat Lawanson.
[8] "Morphology," Dr. Cristina D'Alessandro
[9] "Africa's Rising Urban and Water Population," John F. May.
[10] Ibid.
[11] "Navigating The Impacts Of Climate Change," Hellen Njoki Wanjohi-Opil.
[12] "What Are The Sustainable Development Goals (SDGS)?" SDG Center for Africa. Accessed March 5, 2023. https://sdgcafrica.org/about/the-sdgs/.
[13] "Africa's Youth Renew Commitment to the Sdgs | Africa Renewal." United Nations. United Nations. Accessed March 5, 2023. https://www.un.org/africarenewal/magazine/january-2022/africa%E2%80%99s-youth-renew-commitment-sdgs.
[14] "Growing With the Tide: African Water Cities in the Climate Emergency," Dr Joy Antonia Kategekwa.
[15] "The AFCFTA, an Opportunity for Africa's Youth to Accelerate Trade and Industrialization." The AfCFTA, an opportunity for Africa's youth to accelerate trade and industrialization | United Nations Economic Commission for Africa, January 16, 1970. https://www.uneca.org/stories/the-afcfta%2C-an-opportunity-for-africa%E2%80%99s-youth-to-accelerate-trade-and-industrialization.

BIBLIOGRAPHY

CREDITS

Kunlé Adeyemi
Kunlé Adeyemi is an architect, professor, and development strategist whose works are internationally recognized for originality and innovation. He is the Founding Partner of NLÉ —an architecture, design and urbanism practice founded in 2010, for innovating cities and communities. Adeyemi's notable works include 'Makoko Floating System (MFS™)'—a ground-breaking, prefabricated, building solution for developments on water—deployed in five countries across three continents, with the latest iteration being Mansa Floating Hub in Sao Vicente, Cape Verde. This acclaimed project is part of NLÉ's extensive body of work and new venture—Water Cities® and the African Water Cities Centre—focused on the intersections of rapid urbanization and climate change. Other projects include A Prelude to The Shed in New York, USA, the Black Rhino Academy in Karatu, Tanzania and the Serpentine Summer House at the Royal Kensington Gardens in London, UK. Before founding NLÉ, Adeyemi worked closely with Rem Koolhaas for about nine years at the world renowned Office for Metropolitan Architecture (OMA), where he led the design and development of significant projects such as the Shenzhen Stock Exchange tower in China, the Qatar National Library and Qatar Foundation Headquarters in Doha, Samsung Museum of Art and the Prada Transformer in Seoul. Alongside his professional practice, which has won multiple prestigious awards— Adeyemi is an international speaker and thought leader. He is one of UNDP's Africa in Development Supergroup members. Adeyemi is currently an Adjunct Visiting Professor at the University of Lagos, following appointments in various institutions including Harvard, Princeton, Cornell and Columbia Universities, where he leads academic research in architecture and urban solutions that are closer to societal, environmental and economic needs

Ahunna Eziakonwa
Ahunna Eziakonwa is the UNDP Regional Director for Africa since 2018. She leads UNDP's work supporting 46 countries in Africa to achieve Agenda 2030 and the Sustainable Development Goals. Ms. Eziakonwa has many years of distinguished service with the United Nations, most recently as UN Resident Coordinator and UNDP Resident Representative in Ethiopia since 2015. Before that, she served as Resident Coordinator in Uganda and Lesotho, and held several posts with the Office for Coordination of Humanitarian Affairs (OCHA), as Chief of the Africa Section in New York and in a number of field duty stations (Liberia, Sierra Leone)

Suzanne Lettieri
Suzanne Lettieri is an Assistant Professor in the Department of Architecture at Cornell University and a licensed architect practicing as co-principle of Jefferson Lettieri Office. Her work tackles a range of scales and links image-culture and related technologies to socially conscious design. Lettieri was a University of Michigan Mellon Design Fellow in Egalitarianism and the Metropolis, where she was the lead instructor for ArcPrep, an immersive pre-college programme for Detroit Public High School students. Additionally, she served as an Assistant Professor at the Fashion Institute of Technology, where she initiated the pilot programme 'Inclusive Recruitment Strategies.' She has been awarded a MacDowell fellowship and a Graham Foundation grant and was named a Faculty Fellow in Engaged Scholarship.

Berend Strijland
Berend Strijland is an architect and partner at NLÉ, managing a team of architects on a day-to-day basis in the Amsterdam office. He has worked on the design and development of a wide range of acclaimed projects, such as the Serpentine Summer House 2016, Black Rhino Academy, Prelude to the Shed, and Makoko Floating System in Lagos, Nigeria as well as the later versions in Venice, Bruges, Chengdu and Mindelo. Recent works include a cultural installation in the Netherlands, educational and healthcare facilities in Zimbabwe, and a hotel, sports and commercial complex in Rwanda. He has lectured at institutions such as LUMA Arles, SAIC Chicago and Harvard GSD amongst others, studied at the UIC Chicago School of Architecture and holds a degree from Technical University Delft in Architecture and Building Engineering.

CONTRIBUTORS

Irit Ittner
Irit Ittner's work centers around environmental governance and spontaneous urbanization. Research in Abidjan was implemented during two projects at the University of Bonn, Germany (Waterfront Metropolis Abidjan, 2017-2020, funded by DFG, EG 381/1-1; Urban Villages by the Airport in Mumbai and Abidjan, 2020-2023, funded by Fritz-Thyssen Foundation 10.20.2.003.EL). Irit is employed at the German Institute of Development and Sustainability (IDOS).

John F. May, PhD
John F. May, is a specialist of population policies. He is currently an Assistant Professor at Georgetown University in Washington, DC.

Cristina D'Alessandro
Research Associate Professor Cristina D'Alessandro is a Senior Fellow at the Centre on Governance at the University of Ottawa (Canada), and a Research Fellow at the PRODIG Research Centre, at the University of Paris 1 Sorbonne. Prof. D'Alessandro is widely published in English, French, and Italian. Her research focus is urban planning, management and transformation; natural resources and environmental governance; political, economic and territorial governance; institutional capacity building and leadership.

Steven Mithen
Steven Mithen is a professor of Early Prehistory at the University of Reading

Hellen Njoki Wanjohi-Opil
Hellen Wanjohi-Opil is a spatial planner and climate change expert based out of Nairobi, Kenya. She currently serves as the Resilience Africa Cities Lead, at the World Resources Institute's Africa office (WRI-Africa).

Winnie V. Mitullah
Winne V. Mitullah is a research professor & UNESCO UNITWIN Chair at Institute for Development Studies, University of Nairobi

Prof Chris Changwe Nshimbi, PhD
SARChI Research Chair in the Political Economy of Migration in the SADC Region, Centre for the Study of Governance Innovation (GovInn), Department of Political Sciences, University of Pretoria

Dr Joy Antonia Kategekwa
Dr. Joy Kategekwa is Strategy Advisor on Africa at UNDP's Regional Bureau for Africa. The views expressed herein are the product of analytical and scholarly work. They do not reflect the views of UNDP or its Member States.

Taibat Lawanson
Taibat Olaitan Lawanson is a professor of urban management and governance at the University of Lagos, Nigeria, where she leads the Pro-Poor Development Research Cluster.

Denis W. Aheto
Denis W. Aheto, Professor of Coastal ecology and Director of the Centre for Coastal Management - The Africa Centre of Excellence in Coastal Resilience, University of Cape Coast, Ghana

Peter Kristensen
Lead Environmental Specialist, Environment, Natural Resources, and the Blue Economy Global Practice, The World Bank
For more information, please contact Madjiguene Seck, external affairs and partnership coordinator, The World Bank.

Dr Vincent N. Ojeh
Dr. Vincent N. Ojeh is a Fellow at ARIN. He is also a lecturer with the Department of Geography, Taraba State University, Jalingo, Nigeria.

Ngozi Finette Unuigbe and Violet Omon Aigbokhaevbo
Ngozi F. Unuigbe is a specialist in Environmental Policy, Law, and Ethics

NLÉ / African Water Cities Team
Shruti Maliwar
Dhara Mittal
Shruti Maliwar
Erik Tsurumaki
Daria Borovyk
Victoria Oshinusi
Zakariyya Zango

African Water Cities Academic Research Studios

University of Lagos 2021
Nigeria: 'African Water Cities Center' at the University of Lagos

Princeton University 2019
Cape Verde: 'Cultural Production in African Water Cities' examines the role of architecture at the intersection of cultural developments and environmental conditions of Sao Vicente Island of Cape Verde, West Africa.

Harvard University 2017
South Africa: 'Building Industries in African Water Cities' explores the city of Durban to examine the challenges and opportunities presented by the impacts of urbanization in the social, physical, and environmental context of the African continent.

Columbia University 2016
Côte d'Ivoire: 'Industrialisation in African Water Cities' examines the notion of industrialisation in the production of architecture, infrastructure and Urbanism in the city of Abidjan.

Cornell University 2015
Nigeria: Water & The City II Program: Architecture, Design & Urban Research Studio on Lagos.

Cornell University 2014
Tanzania: Water & The City I Program: Architecture, Design & Urban research Studio on African Cities with focus on Dar es Salaam.

Infrastructure
By Denis W. Aheto & Peter Kristensen

[1] Croitoru, L., Miranda, J., & Sarraf, M (2019). THE COST OF COASTAL ZONE DEGRADATION IN WEST AFRICA: BENIN, CÔTE D'IVOIRE, SENEGAL AND TOGO. https://documents1.worldbank.org/curated/en/8224215525046658 3pdf/The-Cost-of-Coastal-Zone-Degradation-in-West-Africa-Benin-Cote-dIvoire-Senegal-and-Togo.pdf https://documents.worldbank.org/curated/en/822421552504665834/pdf/135269-Madji-49741-WACA-COE Report-Web-March-13.pdf

[2] West Africa's Coast: Losing Over $3. Billion a Year to Erosion, Flooding and Pollution. (2019). World Bank. https://www.worldbank.org/en/region/afr/publication/west-africas-coast-losing-over-38-billion-a-year-to-erosion-flooding-and-pollution https://www.worldbank.org/en/region/afr/publication/west-africas-coast-losing-over-38-billion-a-year-to-erosion-flooding-and-pollution

[3] Niang, I., Ruppel, O. C., Abdrabo, M. A., Essel, C., Lennard, C., Padgham, J., Urquhart, P., & Descheemaeker, K. K. E. (2014). Chapter 22 : Africa. In V. R. Barros, C. B. Field, D. J. Dokken, M. D. Mastrandrea, & K. J. Mach (Eds.), Climate Change 2014: Impacts, Adaptation, and Vulnerability. Part B: Regional Aspects. Contribution of Working Group II to the Fifth Assessment (pp. 1199-1265). (Intergovernmental Panel on Climate Change).. https://doi.org/10.1017/CBO9781107415386.0023] Climate Change 2014. Niang et al., 2014

[4] PENAf. (n.d.).Retrieved May 26, 2023 from https://www.penaf.org/ https://www.penaf.org/

[5] EcoPorts. (n.d.).https://www.ecoports.com/ https://www.ecoports.com/

[6] Green Marine. (2014). https://green-marine.org/

[7][8] Africa Centre of Excellence in Coastal Resilience (ACECoR). (2016, December 21). https://acecor.ucc.edu.gh/

MAP DATA

7 Climate Change Vulnerability Index-Adapted from Verisk Maplecroft (2018)

8-9 Climate Impact Risk- Adapted from European Commission, 'INFORM Climate Change Risk Index all scenario (2023) Online. Available: https://drmkc.jrc.ec.europa.eu/inform-index/INFORM-Climate-Change/INFORM-Climate-Change-Tool

8-9 World Population Growth Rate (%) until 2100- Adapted from United Nations, World Population Prospects 2022. Online. Available at: https://population.un.org/wpp/

16-17 The True Size of Africa- Adapted from Neil R Kaye, 'World Mercator Projection with true size added'(2018) Online. Available at: https://www.reddit.com/r/dataisbeautiful/comments/9nkg7k/map_projections_can_be_deceptive_oc

51 African Urban Centers Population 2050- Adapted from D. Hoornweg, K. Pope, 'Socioeconomic Pathways and Regional Distribution of the World's 101 Largest Cities', Global Cities Institute working Paper No.04 (2014) [online] Available at: https://shared.ontariotechu.ca/shared/faculty-sites/sustainability-today/publications/population-predictions-of-the-101-largest-cities-in-the-21st-century.pdf

61 No. of deaths from floods 2008 -2018 Total- Adapted from Our World n Data 'Number of deaths from floods annual total) 2008-2018', Our World n Data based on EM-DAT, CRED / JCLouvain, Brussels, Belgium – www. emdat.be (D. Guha-Sapir) [online] Available at: https://ourworldindata. rg/natural-disasters

61 Global Internal Displacement aused by floods, storms and wet mass novements 2008-2018 Total- Adapted rom IDMC [online] Available at: https:// www.internal-displacement.org/ database/displacement-data Water Depletion- Adapted from Brauman, KA, B Richter, S Postel, M Malby, M Flörke, 'Water depletion: An improved metric for incorporating seasonal and dry-year water scarcity into water risk assessments', Elementa: Science of the Anthropocene 2016 doi: 10.12952/journal. elementa.000083.f001

SIMER

mographics
97 Birth Rate (per 1,000 people) 2021-Adapted from United Nations, 'Crude Birth Rate (births per 1,000 population)', Population Division (2022) [online] Available at: https://ourworldindata. org/grapher/crude-birth-rate?tab=chart
97 Urban population growth (annual %) 2021 - Adapted from World Bank staff estimates based on the United Nations Population Division's World Urbanization Prospects: 2018 Revision. ' Urban population growth (annual %)- Sub-Saharan Africa', [online] Available at: https://data.worldbank.org/indicator/ SP.URB.GROW?locations=ZG&name_ desc=false.
97 Most Populous city per Country 2021- Adapted from World Population Review. ' Africa Cities by Population 2023'. [online] Available at: https:// worldpopulationreview.com/ continents/africa/cities.
97 Population Density (people per sq/km) 2020- Adapted from UN Food and Agriculture Organization (FAO), Population density in Africa'(2020). [online] Available at: https://www. theglobaleconomy.com/rankings/ population_density/Africa/

onomics
6-107 Economic Growth, Change of Real GDP (Average Annual %) 2005-2020- Adapted from The World Bank Economic growth: the rate of change of real GDP, 2021', TheGlobalEconomy. com [online] Available at: https://www. theglobaleconomy.com/rankings/ Economic_growth/.
6-107 Foreign Direct Investment, net (BoP, currency US$) 2020 - Adapted from International Monetary Fund, Balance of Payments Statistics Yearbook and data files. 'Foreign direct investment, net (BoP, current US$) (BN.KLT.DINV.CD)'[online] Available at: https://databank.worldbank.org/ reports.aspx?source=2&series=BN.KLT. DINV.CD&country
6-107 GDP per Capita (PPP US$) 2021-Adapted from The World Bank 'GDP per capita, Purchasing Power Parity, 2021', [online] Available at: https:// www.theglobaleconomy.com/rankings/ GDP_per_capita_PPP/.
6-107 Inflation, GDP Deflector (annual %) 2020- Adapted from World Bank national accounts and OECD National Accounts, 'Inflation, GDP deflator (annual %)' [online] Available at: https:// data.worldbank.org/indicator/NY.GDP. DEFL.KD.ZG?end=2020&start=2005

ocio-politics
6-117 Corruption, Perceived Least Corrupt Public Sector (index /100) 2021- Adapted from Transparency International 'Corruption Perceptions Index 2021. [online] Available at: https:// www.transparency.org/en/cpi/2021.

116-117 Covid-19 Containment and Health, Government Response Stringency (index /100) 2022 - Adapted from T. Hale, N. Angrist, R. Goldszmidt. et al. 'A global panel database of pandemic policies (Oxford COVID-19 Government Response Tracker)'. Nat Hum Behav 5, 529–538 (2021) https://doi.org/10.1038/ s41562-021-01079-8, Retrieved from: https://ourworldindata.org/grapher/ covid-containment-and-health-index
116-117 Internal Displacement Caused by Conflict 2021- Adapted from IDMC, '2021 Global Report on Internal Displacement'. [online] Available at: https://www.internal-displacement. org/global-report/grid2021/.
116-117 Gender Equality (index/1) 2021-Adapted from World Economic Forum 'Global Gender Gap Report 2022 - Insight Report July 2022'. [online] Available at: https://www.weforum. org/reports/global-gender-gap-report-2022/

Infrastructure
126-127 CO₂ Emissions from Transport (tonnes of CO₂e per capita) 2019-Adapted from Our World in Data based on Climate Analysis Indicators Tool (CAIT) 'Per capita CO2 emissions from transport'. [online] Available at: https:// ourworldindata.org/grapher/per-capita-co2-transport
126-127 Logistics Performance, Quality of Trade and Transport-Related Infrastructure Index/5) 2018- Adapted from The World Bank and Turku School of Economics (2018). 'Logistics performance index: Quality of trade and transport-related infrastructure (1=low to 5=high)' [online] Available at: https:// data.worldbank.org/indicator/LP.LPI. INFR.XQ?locations=CV&most_recent_ year_desc=true&view=map
126-127 Container Port Traffic (20 foot equivalent units)2020- Adapted from UNCTAD 'Container port traffic (TEU: 20 foot equivalent units)' [online] Available at: https://data.worldbank.org/ indicator/IS.SHP.GOOD.TU
126-127 Individuals using the Internet (% of population)2020- Adapted from International Telecommunication Union (ITU) World Telecommunication/ ICT Indicators Database, 'Individuals using the Internet (% of population)'. [online] Available at: https://data. worldbank.org/indicator/IT.NET.USER. ZS?view=map&year=2020/

Morphology
136-137 Elevation Above Sea Level, Most Populous City per Country (m) 2023 - Adapted from Google Earth. [online] Available at: https://earth.google.com
136-137 Access to Electricity (% of population) 2020- Adapted from World Bank Global Electrification Database 'Access to electricity (% of population), 'Tracking SDG 7: The Energy Progress Report [online] Available at: https:// data.worldbank.org/indicator/EG.ELC. ACCS.ZS?view=map.
136-137 Population Living in Slums (% of urban population) 2020- Adapted from United Nations Human Settlements Programme (UN-HABITAT), 'Population living in slums (% of urban population)'. [online] Available at: https://data. worldbank.org/indicator/EN.POP. SLUM.UR.ZS?end=2020&start= 2020&view=map
136-137 Population Living in Urban Areas (% of population) 2020- Adapted from UN Population Division (via World Bank). 'Share of people living in urban areas, 2020'. Available at: https:// ourworldindata.org/grapher/share-of-population-urban

Environment
146-147 Annual Precipitation (mm per year) 2019- Adapted from UN Food and Agriculture Organization, 'Average precipitation in depth (mm per year) - Sub-Saharan Africa'.[online] Available at: https://data.worldbank. org/indicator/AG.LND.PRCP. MM?end =2020&locations=ZG&start= 2020&view=map&year=2019

146-147 Flood & Storm Disaster Events 2020-2021 / Internal Displacement Caused by Floods & Storms 2020-2021-Adapted from IDMC. [online] Available at: https://www.internal-displacement. org/database/displacement-data.
146-147 Population Physically Exposed to Flooding (index /10) 2022- Adapted from Statista. 'Africa: flood risk 2022'. [online] Available at: https://www.statista.com/ statistics/1313372/physical-exposure-to-floods-by-country-africa/

Resources
156-157 Land Covered by Forest (% of Land area) 2020- Adapted from UN Food and Agriculture Organization (FAO). Forest Resources Assessment 2020. 'Share of land covered by forest 2020'. [online] Available at: https:// ourworldindata.org/grapher/forest-area-as-share-of-land-area
156-157 Water Stress (% of freshwater withdrawal compared to available freshwater sources) 2019- Adapted from UN Food and Agriculture Organization (FAO) 'Level of water stress: freshwater withdrawal as a proportion of available freshwater resources' [online] Available at: https://www.fao.org/sustainable-development-goals/indicators/642/ en/#:~:text=The%20level%20of%20 water%20stress .
156-157 Income from natural resources, (% of GDP) 2020- Adapted from The World Bank, 'Income from natural resources, percent of GDP, 2020' [online] Available at: https://www.theglobaleconomy. com/rankings/Natural_resources_ income/
156-157 Agricultural Raw Material Exports (% of merchandise exports) 2017-2021- Adapted from World Bank staff estimates through the WITS platform from the Comtrade database maintained by the United Nations Statistics Division, ' Agricultural raw materials exports (% of merchandise exports)' [online] Available at: https://data.worldbank.org/ indicator/TX.VAL.AGRI.ZS.UN
173 Deaths and Displacements across African Cities- Adapted from Floodlist. [online] Available at: https://floodlist. com/

[Websites Accessed 3 Apr. 2023]

PHOTO CREDITS

Cover: Photo: ©Yann Arthus-Bertrand. Makoko, Lagos Lagoon, Lagos State, Nigeria (6°30' N - 3°24' E).
2-3 NLÉ, Olalekan Jeyifous
12-13 Olumide Oresegun
4-5, 44-45,53, 70-71, 115, 125, 216-217, 229, 260, 263 NLÉ
20-21, 32-41, 216-217 Iwan Baan
26-27 Calida Rawles
28 ByValet
31 Elena Ska
42-43 Malik Afegbua
46 Siegfried Modola
52 CDR International
55 Emmanuel Iwuegbu
57 MT CUrado
58-59 Jacque Njeri
64-65 Library of Congress, Prints & Photographs Division, [LC-USZ62-38346]
66-67 Rafael Almar
67, 69, 71, 73, 75, 249 Google Earth Pro 2022
68-69, 244 Donnish Pewee. Courtesy of iLab Liberia
72-73 Gilles Comlanvi
74-75 Helge Denker
76 Tim Wege
79 Roger Hutchings
80 Cynthia Morinville
83 Opare Manu / Wikimedia Commons
86-87 Wilfred Ukpong
92-93 Rogan Ward
95 Daniel Omolewa
98 Ade Olagunju
102-103 Frederic Noy
105 Keren Su
108 Valeriy Tretyakov
111 Philip Mostert
112-113 Peeter Viisimaa
118 MT Curado

121 Omoregie Osakpolor
122-123 Iwaria Inc.
128 Eugene Sergeev
132-133 Jeroen van Loon
135, 248 Helge Denker
138 Hirlesteanu Dumitru
142-143 Almohimen Sayed
145 Mariusz Prusaczyk
147 Arafat Jamal
152-153 Brent Stirton
155 Marcus Wilson-Smith
158 Joerg Boethling
161 DeAgostini
162-163 Stamp Cabo Verde
170-171 Radu Sigheti
172 Adou Innocent Kouadio, Gkbediako/ wikicommons, Afhunta, Vincent Lali/ GroundUp, Birgit Korber, Theresa Carpenter/ Flickr, MyriamLouviot, Ilya Varlamov/Flickr, Dale Hancock, Jameswasswa / Wiki Commons, Radio Okapi/ Flickr, Tolu Owoeye, Elodie Toto/mongabay.com, Alan Gignoux, Llucky78/Dreamstime, Tarikh Jumeer, UNEP
174 Djebi Abraham Philips
175, 177, 179, 182, 184, 186, 188, 193, 197, 205 Unsplash
176 Kwame Appah
178 MT Curado
180 Dmitrii Pichugin
181 Abaca Press
183 Arild Lilleboe
185 Faris Knight/ Wikipedia
187 Karabo Mduli
189 Pixabay
190 Benindronelab
191 Junior Samson
192 Derejeb
194 ha niceEmiliano Gandolfi/ Wikimedia Commons
195, 243 Mtcurado
196 Leonardo Viti
198 David Keith Jones
199 Rise Images
200 Zozo/Panther Media GmbH
201 Marie Cacace
202 Nupo Deyon Daniel
203 Namnso Ukpanah
204 Robert Ross / Gallo Images
206 Kostadin Luchansky
207 Harmeneglido Sebastian
208, 209 jbdodane
210 Sapsiwai
211 John Barratt
212 Roland And Elena Obermeier
213 Hansueli Krapf
226-227, 230 Kriolscope
231 Dave Saunders
232 Rafael Almar (IRD/LEGOS, 10 dec 2016]
233 Agencia Anadolu
234 Terraforce
235 David Steele
236 Ath Salem
237 Aimable Twahirwa
238 Urbaplan
239 TenCate
240 Photovs
241 Inros Lackner
242 Moussa Diarra/World Bank
245 Irit Eguavon
246 UNHCR/Charlotte Hallqvist
247 NORCAP
250 Taarifa News
251 World Bank
252 Annika Seifert
253 Roshni Lodhia
258-259 Alun Be

CREDITS

Author: Kunlé Adeyemi
Foreword: Ahunna Eziakonwa
Editors: Suzanne Lettieri, Berend Strijland
Copy editing: Leo Reijnen
Design: Studio Sander Boon
Printing and lithography:
NPN Drukkers
Paper: Munken Lynx Rough 120 gr
Publisher: Marcel Witvoet,
nai010 publishers

This publication was made possible
by financial support from
The Graham Foundation, Creative
Industries Fund NL, NLÉ, Water Cities®

Although every effort was made to find the
copyright holders for the illustrations used,
it has not been possible to trace them all.
Interested parties are requested to contact
nai010 publishers, Korte Hoogstraat 31,
3011 GK Rotterdam, the Netherlands.

nai010 publishers is an internationally
orientated publisher specialized in
developing, producing and distributing
books in the fields of architecture,
urbanism, art and design. www.nai010.com

nai010 books are available internationally at
selected bookstores and from the following
distribution partners:

North, Central and South America -
Artbook | D.A.P., New York, USA,
dap@dapinc.com

Rest of the world - Idea Books, Amsterdam,
the Netherlands, idea@ideabooks.nl

For general questions, please contact
nai010 publishers directly at sales@nai010.
com or visit our website www.nai010.com
for further information.

Printed and bound in the Netherlands

ISBN 978-94-6208-776-7

NUR 648
BISAC ARC010000, ARC020000
THEMA AMVD